Essential
Thailand

AAA Publishing 1000 AAA Drive, Heathrow, Florida 32746

Thailand: Regions and Best places to see

 Best places to see 34–55

 Central Thailand 85–122

Southern Thailand 123–146

■ Featured sight

 Northern Thailand 147–172

 Isaan 173–187

Original text by Andrew Forbes and David Henley

American editor: G.K. Sharman

Edited, designed and produced by AA Publishing
© Automobile Association Developments Limited 2007
Maps © Automobile Association Developments Limited 2007

ISBN-13: 978-1-59508-190-2
ISBN-10: 1-59508-190-9

Published in the United States by AAA Publishing,
1000 AAA Drive, Heathrow, Florida 32746
Published in the United Kingdom by AA Publishing

Colour separation: MRM Graphics Ltd
Printed and bound in Italy by Printer Trento S.r.l.

A02694
Maps in this title produced from map data © New Holland Publishing (South Africa)
(Pty) Ltd. 2005
Transport map © Communicarta Ltd, UK

About this book

Symbols are used to denote the following categories:

- map reference to maps on cover
- address or location
- telephone number
- opening times
- admission charge
- restaurant or café on premises or nearby
- nearest underground train station
- nearest bus/tram route
- nearest overground train station
- nearest ferry stop
- nearest airport
- other practical information
- tourist information office
- indicates the page where you will find a fuller description

This book is divided into five sections.

The essence of Thailand pages 6–19
Introduction; Features; Food and Drink; Short Break including the 10 Essentials

Planning pages 20–33
Before You Go; Getting There; Getting Around; Being There

Best places to see pages 34–55
The unmissable highlights of any visit to Thailand

Best things to do pages 56–81
Good places to have lunch; great adventures; stunning views; best shopping; places to take the children and more

Exploring pages 82–187
The best places to visit in Thailand, organized by area

Maps
All map references are to the maps on the covers. For example, Ko Tao has the reference ☩ 15N – indicating the grid square in which it is to be found.

Prices
An indication of the cost of restaurants and cafés at attractions is given by **B** (baht) signs: **BBB** denotes higher prices, **BB** denotes average prices, **B** denotes lower prices.

Hotel prices
Per room per night: **B** budget (under B1,000); **BB** moderate (B1,000–2,500); **BBB** expensive (over B2,500)

Restaurant prices
A three-course meal per person without drinks: **B** budget (under B200); **BB** moderate (B200–500); **BBB** expensive (over B500)

Contents

BEST THINGS TO DO

56 – 81

EXPLORING...

82 – 187

The essence of...

Nation, religion and monarchy are the cornerstones of life in Thailand. Thais are passionate about their country in a mellow and heartfelt way. They invariably stand when the national anthem is played and adore their royal family. The influence of Theravada Buddhism is also pervasive; throughout the country, monks' soft chanting and temple bells fill the air.

In a country renowned for its wild nightlife, Thais can be extremely modest – revealing clothing and nude sunbathing are not acceptable – and yet general attitudes are also astonishingly liberal in many ways.

features

Thailand is a fortunate country. Its name means 'Land of the Free' and, almost alone in Asia, it has escaped colonization by the West. Fertile, warm, washed by the seas of both the Indian and the Pacific oceans and with a people well known for their friendliness, the country completely lives up to its popular sobriquet 'Land of Smiles'. From the mountainous north to the jewel-like islands of the south, the scenery is breathtaking.

Thailand is not just a delight for hedonists. This ancient kingdom has produced some of the most outstanding architecture in the world, from the Grand Palace in Bangkok to the temple-studded city of Chiang Mai in the north. Saffron-clad Buddhist monks, colourful minority hill tribes and the general population bear daily witness to Thailand's age-old culture and traditions. They form a vibrant backdrop for adventurous pursuits such as elephant riding, trekking and diving. Exciting nightlife, delicious cuisine and world-class shopping ensure this destination satisfies every taste and purpose.

GEOGRAPHY

Thailand is generally divided geographically into four areas: the mountainous north, the vast arid plateau of the northeast, the

flat central plains dominated by Bangkok, and the peninsular south, famous for its beaches.

POPULATION
More than twice the size of the United Kingdom and with a similar population size, Thailand is still predominantly rural – outside Bangkok.

THE CAPITAL
Bangkok's population is around 10 million. It is 30 times larger than any other Thai city and dominates the nation's economic, political and cultural life.

THE PEOPLE
Thai (and closely related Lao) people make up more than 75 per cent of the country's 62 million inhabitants. There is a well-integrated ethnic Chinese minority (about 11 per cent), Malay-speaking Muslims in the deep south (5 per cent), roughly two million native Cambodian speakers in the northeast, and members of around a dozen hill tribes in the north and west.

NATURE
Thailand has a large number of national parks and wildlife sanctuaries. Some of these lie surprisingly close to Bangkok, including Khao Yai, one of the largest tropical monsoon forests in Asia. More than 50km (31 miles) of hiking trails offer access to wild elephants, sambar deer, Malayan sun bears, Asiatic black bears and diverse bird life.

ISLAND LIFE
The Gulf of Siam and Andaman Sea are dotted with many almost deserted islands. In contrast to well-developed resort islands such as Phuket and Ko Samui some, such as Ko Chang, retain a pristine, Robinson Crusoe atmosphere.

food & drink

Popular in the West for the past 20 years, Thai cuisine ranks beside French, Italian and Chinese as one of the most highly esteemed in the world. The good news is that Thai food is much more reasonably priced in Thailand than back home.

RICE

Rice is central to most Thai meals, although the national fondness for noodles shows the strength of Chinese influence. Thais eat two kinds of rice: slightly fluffy, long-grain rice, eaten with a spoon and fork; and sticky rice, eaten with the fingers. Noodles are always eaten with chopsticks.

MEAT

Meat is generally stir-fried or otherwise cooked in bite-sized pieces, which explains the absence of knives on Thai tables. Thai pork is among the best in the world; chicken and duck are also excellent. Beef is widely available but can be a little tough.

Consumption of lamb, mutton and goat is largely limited to Thailand's Muslim community.

FISH AND SEAFOOD

Fresh and saltwater fish, shrimp, lobsters, crabs, clams, mussels, squid and octopuses are all available. The best place to enjoy fresh seafood is by the sea but even Chiang Mai, amid the northern mountains, has excellent fresh seafood flown and trucked in daily. Imported varieties of fish have become increasingly available in Thailand; it is not surprising to find smoked salmon from Scotland or Norwegian herring on the menu.

FRUIT AND VEGETABLES

Fresh fruit and vegetables are available throughout the country, from temperate crops such as asparagus, celery, apples and strawberries grown in the cool north to more exotic varieties such as rambutan, mangosteen, durian, pineapple,

mango and tamarind that flourish in the warmer tropics. In recent years avocados have been introduced from Israel and kiwi fruit from New Zealand. Moreover, anything that does not grow in Thailand with ease – such as cherries, walnuts, nectarines and apricots – is flown in regularly and available on supermarket shelves or in restaurants.

DRINK

Bottled, purified water and a wide range of internationally known soft drinks are available everywhere – even in remote places. Thailand produces several good (but strong) local brews

including Singha (Lion) and Chang (Elephant) beers. International brands such as San Miguel and Heineken are brewed locally under licence. There is a plethora of local whiskies and rums and everything that can be imported is imported, from the best Russian vodka to the top Scotch malt. Thais have recently discovered a taste for wine, too, and import widely, although mainly from Australia and South America.

MEALTIMES

Whatever, whenever. Thais eat when they are hungry and do not understand the Western concept of fixed mealtimes. They tend to eat less than Westerners but more frequently. That said, all hotels and restaurants catering to foreign visitors are aware of the international habit of eating three fixed meals a day and make allowances for it.

short break

If you have only a short time to visit Thailand and would like to take home some unforgettable memories, you can do something local and capture the real flavour of the country. The following suggestions will give you a wide range of sights and experiences that won't take very long, won't cost very much and will make your visit very special.

● **Visit the Grand Palace** Many visitors to Thailand make a stop in the capital. Here, don't miss the gilded Grand Palace (➤ 40–41) and associated temples and museums on Ratanakosin Island, in the heart of Bangkok, which are literally dazzling.

● **See the house of silk entrepreneur, Jim Thompson** On a sleepy backstreet of downtown Bangkok, this delightful amalgamation of traditional Thai wooden buildings houses a collection of Thai, Burmese and Cambodian antiquities (➤ 93). It is a good introduction to the country's ancient tradition of silk weaving, as well as to its building practices.

● **Visit a tropical island** No visitor to the country should miss seeing one of its stunning islands. Thailand has hundreds of the most pristine tropical islands in the world. Choose Phuket (➤ 124–127), Ko Samui (➤ 131) or a less well-developed spot such as Ko Chang (➤ 104).

● **View a Khmer temple** For something a little different, go to Prasat Phanom Rung (➤ 48–49) or Prasat Hin Phimai (➤ 179) – better yet, visit both. These are the world's best-preserved Khmer temples dating from the classical Angkor period, and are well worth a look.

● **Taste Thai food** Thailand has one of the greatest culinary traditions in the world, offering wonderfully good value and high quality 'fast food' for those in a hurry. Because there are no fixed meal times and food is available on practically every corner, you're never far away from a tasty treat.

● **Riverside retreats** Even if you don't have time to get to a beach, you may well find yourself close to a river in Thailand. Both Bangkok's and Chiang Mai's main waterways offer a welcome respite from these bustling cities.

● **See some traditional dancing** Classical Thai dance, rooted in the traditions of classical India, is exquisitely sophisticated. One of the best places to see a performance is at Bangkok's Erawan Shrine (➤ 89) where a traditional Thai orchestra and religious dancers come to life whenever a visitor pays them to do so.

● **Visit a Buddhist temple** A visit to a Thai temple, or wat, where serene monks sit chanting age-old Pali scriptures, is an essential ingredient to understanding the country. Take time to catch even just a glimpse inside a local temple and you will be rewarded with an insight into another world.

● **Explore a Thai market** Local markets are a wonderful way to experience Thailand. Almost any market will do, but for a real experience go to one of the 'floating markets' by boat, such as Bang Khu Wiang (➤ 88) near Bangkok, early in the morning when trading is at its peak. Or, hunt for souvenirs at Chiang Mai's atmospheric night bazaar (➤ 153).

● **Relax with a massage** What better way to round off a flying visit to Thailand, than with a traditional massage? This tension-reducing treatment can be enjoyed anywhere in the country, but Wat Pho (➤ 77) in Bangkok, the national headquarters for massage training, is probably the best place.

Planning

Before You Go

WHEN TO GO

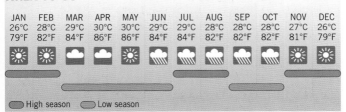

JAN	FEB	MAR	APR	MAY	JUN	JUL	AUG	SEP	OCT	NOV	DEC
26°C	28°C	29°C	30°C	30°C	29°C	29°C	28°C	28°C	28°C	27°C	26°C
79°F	82°F	84°F	86°F	86°F	84°F	84°F	82°F	82°F	82°F	81°F	79°F

High season   Low season

Thailand has three seasons: wet (Jun–Oct), cool (Nov–Feb) and hot (Mar–May). **Temperatures** are generally warm, but it can get cold in the north, especially at night, and very hot in April and May. There are **monsoons** in the north, northeast and central parts of the country.

High season, when the weather is at its most pleasant and when prices are higher and accommodation and transport are fully reserved, is November to February, July and August. **Low season** is March to June, September and October. Monsoon can be a good time to go but it mostly depends on luck; temperatures are more conducive to travel, it is easier to get accommodation and transport and there are fewer tourists around.

WHAT YOU NEED

● Required
○ Suggested
▲ Not required

Some countries require a passport to remain valid for a minimum period (usually at least six months) beyond the date of entry contact their consulate or embassy or your travel agent for details.

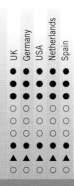

	UK	Germany	USA	Netherlands	Spain
Passport (valid for at least six months beyond period of stay)	●	●	●	●	●
Visa (for periods over one month)	●	●	●	●	●
Onward or Return Ticket	●	●	●	●	●
Health Inoculations (diptheria, tetanus, hep A&B, typhoid)	○	○	○	○	○
Health Documentation (► 23, Health Advice)	○	○	○	○	○
Travel Insurance	○	○	○	○	○
Driving Licence (national)	●	●	●	●	●
Car Insurance Certificate and Registration Document	▲	▲	▲	▲	▲
Proof of funds (sometimes required)	○	○	○	○	○

ADVANCE PLANNING
WEBSITES

● Thailand Tourist Authority: **www.**tourismthailand.org provides a destination guide and online booking service **www.**thaismile.co.uk (UK and Ireland) has information on planning a trip and features on Thailand

TOURIST OFFICES AT HOME

In the UK Tourism Authority of Thailand ✉ 3rd Floor, Brook House, 98–99 Jermyn Street, London SW1Y 6EE ☎ 0870 900 2007

In the USA Tourism Authority of Thailand ✉ 61 Broadway, Suite 2810, New York NY 10006 ☎ 212 432 0433

In Australia Tourism Authority of Thailand ✉ 2nd Floor, 75 Pitt Street, Sydney, NSW 2000 ☎ 02 9247 7549

HEALTH ADVICE

Insurance Visitors are strongly recommended to arrange comprehensive medical insurance before leaving for Thailand. This should include home transport in the event of serious illness, usually included in your travel insurance policy. Medical facilities are generally good, but in the case of severe health problems, contact your embassy and insurance company.

Dental services Private medical insurance, including dental treatment, is advisable. Dental clinics are of a high standard and all major tourist destinations have plenty to choose from, although Bangkok has the best options. Ask your hotel or insurance company for details of contacts, if necessary.

TIME DIFFERENCES

GMT 12 noon	Thailand 7PM	Germany 1PM	USA (NY) 7AM	Netherlands 1PM	Spain 1PM

Thailand is 7 hours ahead of Greenwich Mean Time (GMT+7). There is only one time zone throughout the country. Thailand's position within the tropical zone means that the number of daylight hours varies little over a year.

WHAT'S ON WHEN

Thailand has many festivals and temple fairs, especially between November and February. Dates for festivals vary from year to year, either due to the lunar calendar or local authorities changing the dates.

Chinese New Year in January or February is not a public holiday, but most shops close.

January *Don Chedi Memorial Fair*, Suphanburi: commemorates King Naresuan's victory over Burmese invaders in 1592.
Bor Sang Umbrella Fair and *San Kampaeng Handicrafts Festival*, near Chiang Mai

February *Flower Festival*, Chiang Mai: includes a lively parade.
Phra Nakhon Khiri Diamond Festival, Phetchaburi: celebrates local history.
Chinese New Year, Nakhon Sawan: Chinese New Year festivities at their most exuberant.
Elephant Kantoke Fair, Lampang: elephants are treated to a feast.

March *ASEAN Barred Ground Dove Fair*, Yala: dove-cooing contest featuring contestants from Southeast Asia.
International Jewellery Fair, Bangkok: features buyers and sellers from around the world.
Phanom Rung Festival: light shows and processions celebrate the history of this Khmer temple.
Phra Phutthabaat Festival, Saraburi: pilgrimage to Wat Phra Phutthabaat.

April *Songkhran,* Thailand's New Year festival: originally a festival for anointing the Buddha image with holy water, but now involves three-day street 'battles' where revellers douse each other with water.

Mid-May to mid-June *Phi Ta Khon Festival,* Loei (Dan Sai district): animist-Buddhist celebration with wild masks and costumes.
Rocket Festival, Yasothon (and all over the northeast): huge, home-made rockets are launched to bring rain to the rice fields.

NATIONAL HOLIDAYS

JAN	FEB	MAR	APR	MAY	JUN	JUL	AUG	SEP	OCT	NOV	DEC
1	1		2	3		1	1		1		3

1 January	New Year's Day
February	Magha Puja
6 April	Chakri Day
13–15 April	Songkran
1 May	Labour Day
5 May	Coronation Day
May	Visakha Puja
July	Asanha Puja
12 August	Queen's Birthday
23 October	King Chulalongkorn Day
5 December	King's Birthday
10 December	Constitution Day
31 December	New Year's Eve

Most shops and department stores are open during national holidays.

Royal Ploughing Ceremony, Bangkok: ancient Brahman ritual held at Sanam Luang.

July *Candle Festival*, Ubon Ratchathani (and all over the northeast): candle parade.

September
International Swan-Boat Races, Bangkok: on the Chao Phraya River.
Narathiwat Fair, Narathiwat: a week celebrating southern culture. Features boat races.

October *Vegetarian Festival*, Phuket: nine days of feasting plus acts of self-mortification to the nine emperor gods of Taoism.

November *Loy Krathong*, whole country (best in the north and Sukhothai): on full-moon night, small lotus-shaped baskets with flowers and candles are floated on rivers, lakes and canals.
Elephant Roundup, Surin: elephants play football, re-enact battles and roll logs, among other feats.

Late November to early December *River Kwai Bridge Week*, Kanchanaburi: includes nightly sound-and-light shows.

Getting There

BY AIR

At the time of writing, Bangkok's new international airport, Suvarnabhumi, was expected to open in September 2006. The opening date has been subject to numerous delays. Suvarnabhumi airport is 25km (15 miles) east of the city on the road to Pattaya and the Eastern Seaboard. The old airport, Don Muang, will become a military airfield.

A comprehensive national air service, operated by the national carrier, Thai Airways, and several smaller, 'no frills' airlines, connect all the major cities, while Chiang Mai and Phuket have international airports.

Journey times to the city centre

Suvarnabhumi International Airport is located on a new ring road, and transport to the city center should take no more than half an hour, but at peak times (early morning and late afternoon) allow an hour. Chiang Mai Airport is 4km (2 miles) to the city centre, which is a 10-minute taxi ride (no trains or buses are available). Phuket airport, in the north of the island, is no more than a half-hour taxi ride from all the resorts.

Airport facilities Facilities at Bangkok's airport include currency exchanges, a post and telephone communications office and left luggage, all of which are open 24 hours. There is also the Thai Hotel Association reservations service, which can check on vacancies at their member hotels, a tourist office and several restaurants and bars on the upper floors.

Departure tax Note that on leaving Thailand you will be charged a departure tax, currently B500, for which credit cards are not accepted.

From the airport to Bangkok by taxi Travelling by taxi into town from the airport is probably the best choice after a long flight. The journey should take around 30 minutes. Take a licensed cab from the booth outside the Arrivals hall. Ignore any drivers who approach you directly; they may be unlicensed and will almost certainly try to charge you an extortionate fare. You can take taxis with either a fixed fare (make sure you agree the fee in advance) or a meter. There's little difference in price, although in rush hour a metered ride can soon escalate. You will have to pay tolls into the city in addition to the fare, but they should be included in any flat rate quoted.

From the airport to Bangkok by limousine Costing about twice the price of a taxi, taking a limousine is still a relatively reasonably priced option. As well as a little extra luxury, it means you can avoid having to wait for a taxi. Several companies operate from the

airport – ask for details from the Tourism Authority of Thailand office. Make sure you establish a price beforehand.

From the airport to Bangkok by airport bus Much more comfortable, and probably safer than catching the public bus, the airport bus is considerably cheaper than travelling by taxi. Although the chances are it won't take you exactly to your destination, the service does stop at some of the city's larger hotels.

From the airport to Bangkok by train A fast rail link from the new airport to central Bangkok is under construction. Journey time will be about 30 minutes, incorporating stops connecting with Bangkok's underground metro system and the Skytrain (➤ 28–29).

Getting Around

PUBLIC TRANSPORT
INTERNAL FLIGHTS

The national carrier Thai Airways (THAI) and several private airlines link all the major towns and cities within the country. THAI also offers special domestic air passes with reasonable savings, but these need to be purchased outside the country. Fares on the smaller airlines are much less expensive, but in-flight service is minimal.

TRAINS

An efficient rail network covers most of Thailand. A north–south line connects Bangkok with Chiang Mai in the north, and the Malaysian border in the south. A northeastern line runs through the Isaan region to the Laotian border at Nong Khai,

on the Mekong River. Long-distance trains have first- and second-class sleeping accommodation, which is comfortable and clean. Trains have dining cars or a trolley service. Journey times are long (12 hours from Bangkok to Chiang Mai) due to Thailand's narrow gauge.

NATIONAL BUS TRAVEL

To reach certain places in Thailand, your only option may be the orange, non-air-conditioned government buses. These take a long time to reach their destination, stopping at every village en route. Long distances are covered by so-called VIP buses, which are very comfortable; the fare includes the price of a meal at a motorway service station. The services are operated by several private companies and a state-run enterprise, so fares are highly competitive. Tickets are available at travel agencies or bus stations.

URBAN TRANSPORT

Public transport in Bangkok is provided by a very cheap bus service (air-conditioned, non-air-conditioned and mini-buses); a more expensive above-ground

'Skytrain' (stations are signposted BTS) and a new metro network (MRT). Destinations near the Chao Phraya River can be reached by a fast and efficient riverboat service, which travels as far as the northern suburb of Nonthaburi. A fun way to travel through Bangkok's jammed streets is by *tuk-tuk*, the city's famous three-wheeled, two-stroke open taxi; but negotiate the fare before boarding.

TAXIS
Taxis cruise all of Bangkok's major streets. Make sure the meter is switched on at the beginning of a journey. Fares are reasonable, so a small tip is expected. There are few taxis in other parts of the country.

CAR RENTAL
It is possible to rent vehicles in all major tourist destinations through both the large,international rental companies and the smaller, local rental companies. A four-wheel drive is recommended in the north.

DRIVING
Drive on the left.
Speed limit on expressways:
120kph (74mph)
Speed limit on main roads:
100kph (62mph)
Speed limit on urban roads:
50kph (31mph)

Seat belts must be worn in front seats at all times.

Random breath-testing. Never drive under the influence of alcohol.

Fuel comes in unleaded 95 octane and unleaded 91 octane. Diesel is also available. All are sold by the litre. Service stations abound in all the larger towns and cities but be careful to fill up for longer, cross-country journeys.

There are plenty of motor repair garages throughout the country. Most service stations will also be able to offer some help in the event of a breakdown. International car rental companies include a free breakdown service in their rental packages. Most local rental companies provide a breakdown service but will charge a fee.

CONCESSIONS
Students/youths Some museums and guest houses offer reduced rates for holders of International Student Identity Cards (available though STA travel;
www.statravel.com).
Senior citizens There are almost no concessions for seniors, but this is made up for by the way in which the Thais treat older people. Age confers status and respect.

Being There

TOURIST OFFICES

HEAD OFFICE
- Tourism Authority of Thailand (TAT) Head Office ✉ 1600 New Petchaburi Road, Makkasan, Ratchathewi, Bangkok 10400 ☎ 022 505 500

LOCAL OFFICES
Bangkok
- 4 Thanon Ratchadamnoen Nok ☎ 022 282 9773

Chiang Mai
- 105/1 Chiang Mai–Lamphun Road, Chiang Mai 5000 ☎ 053 248 604

Chiang Rai
- Thanon, Singkhlai Chiang Rai 5700 ☎ 053 717 433

Pattaya
- 382/1 Thanon Chaihat, Pattaya City ☎ 038 427 667

- 609 Moo 10, Pratamunk Road, Banglamung, Chonburi 20150 ☎ 038 428 990

Phuket
- 73–75 Phuket Road, Phuket 8300 ☎ 076 211 036

The Tourism Authority of Thailand (TAT) is a government-run tourist information service providing excellent pamphlets on travel and tourism. With more than 20 offices in Thailand and 16 branches overseas, the TAT regulates all tourism-related businesses, cutting out most unscrupulous operators.

EMBASSIES IN BANGKOK
UK: 022 530 191
Germany: 022 856 627
USA: 022 054 000
Netherlands: 022 547 701
Spain: 026 618 284

EMERGENCY TELEPHONE NUMBERS
Police: 191, 193
Tourist Police: 1155
Fire: 199
Ambulance: 191

TELEPHONES
International calls can be made from hotels, airports and clearly

OPENING HOURS

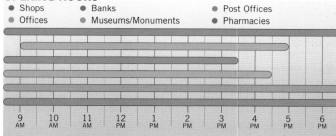

- ● Shops
- ● Offices
- ● Banks
- ● Museums/Monuments
- ● Post Offices
- ● Pharmacies

9 AM | 10 AM | 11 AM | 12 PM | 1 PM | 2 PM | 3 PM | 4 PM | 5 PM | 6 PM

In the larger cities some pharmacies stay open 24 hours. Small shops are usually open by 8.30am and tend to close by 6pm. Department stores open about 10am and close as late as 10pm. The popular 7-Eleven minimarkets are open 24 hours.

Markets open as early as 3am and many are finished by 8am; others stay open until the early afternoon. National museums normally follow the times stated above, but the many privately run museums vary. All government offices, post offices and banks close for national holidays.

identified street call boxes, which take coins or phone cards (available at newsagents, post offices and many shops). Many Internet shops in Bangkok, Chiang Mai and larger cities offer cheap international calls, made via the Internet.

INTERNATIONAL DIALLING CODES

From Thailand dial 001 then:
UK: 44
Germany: 49
USA: 1
Netherlands: 31
Spain: 34

POSTAL SERVICES

The Thai postal service is very efficient and reasonably priced. Registered mail costs an extra B45 per item. There is a post office in every town selling stamps and stationery.

ELECTRICITY

The power supply is: 220 volts, 50 cycles AC.

Plug sockets are usually two flat-pronged terminals or two round-pole terminals. Adaptors can be purchased at any electrical store for all international plug types.

CURRENCY AND FOREIGN EXCHANGE

Currency Thai currency is decimal based and divided into baht (B) and satang. There are 100 satang to 1 baht (B1). Coins now in circulation are in denominations of 25 and 50 satang and in B1, B5 and B10. Notes are in denominations of B10, B20, B50, B100, B500 and B1000.

Exchange Traveller's cheques can be cashed at banks and exchange counters in major towns and resorts.

Credit cards Visa, MasterCard, American Express and Diner's Club are accepted at all luxury hotels and the more expensive restaurants.

HEALTH AND SAFETY

Drugs Most pharmacists in Thailand speak English and pharmacies stay open long hours. Most Western medicine is available but if you are on special or unusual medication, remember to bring supplies with you.

Jewellery scams Many visitors are still taken in by gem tricksters in Bangkok and elsewhere. Beware of unsolicited approaches by people promising special sales or the opportunity to 'buy cheap and sell dear' when you return home.

Mosquitoes Malaria is a problem near the borders with Myanmar (Burma), Cambodia and Laos; in hilly, forested areas and on certain islands, notably Ko Chang. Big cities are safer, although some hotels still offer mosquito nets and it is wise to use a mosquito repellent. Ask your GP for advice about taking anti-malarial tablets.

TIPS/GRATUITIES

Yes ✓   No ✗

Simple restaurants (if service not included)	✓ B20
Expensive restaurants	✓ 10% or more
Hotels and guesthouses (if service not included)	✓ B20 per night
Taxis	✓ round up B20
Porters, room service	✓ B20
Chambermaids	✓ B20 per day
Hairdressers, masseurs	✓ B20
Tour guides	✓ B20
Toilets	✗

Safe water Although city water supplies are chlorinated, avoid drinking tap water. Bottled water is provided in restaurants and can be bought in shops.

Sun advice Sun protection is essential in Thailand. Wear a hat on long walks, especially during the midday hours. Use a high-SPF sunscreen and ensure children are properly protected.

PERSONAL SAFETY

Violent crime is rare, but take the following precautions:
● Lock your hotel room doors and windows at night.
● Don't accept food and drink from strangers on trains and buses; there have been cases of passengers being drugged and robbed.
● The Tourism Aurthority of Thailand (TAT) ➤ 30 or the Tourist Police (☎ 1155) will contact the relevant emergency service and deal with complaints. The operators speak English.

PHOTOGRAPHY

What to photograph: Temples, mountains, festivals, markets, rural life, canal and river life.
Best time to photograph: Between November and March the weather is sunny and clear.

CLOTHING SIZES

Thailand	UK	Rest of Europe	USA	
46	36	46	36	
48	38	48	38	Suits
50	40	50	40	
52	42	52	42	
54	44	54	44	
56	46	56	46	
41	7	41	8	
42	7.5	42	8.5	
43	8.5	43	9.5	Shoes
44	9.5	44	10.5	
45	10.5	45	11.5	
46	11	46	12	
37	14.5	37	14.5	
38	15	38	15	
39/40	15.5	39/40	15.5	Shirts
41	16	41	16	
42	16.5	42	16.5	
43	17	43	17	
36	8	34	6	
38	10	36	8	
40	12	38	10	Dresses
42	14	40	12	
44	16	42	14	
46	18	44	16	
38	4.5	38	6	
38	5	38	6.5	
39	5.5	39	7	Shoes
39	6	39	7.5	
40	6.5	40	8	
41	7	41	8.5	

Best places to see

1

Chatuchak Weekend Market

Almost 9,000 stalls cater to an estimated 500,000 daily visitors at the king of Thai markets.

From endangered wildlife to opium pipes, hill-tribe crafts to herbal remedies, everything is sold at Bangkok's weekend market. Musical instruments, religious amulets, antiques, flowers, clothes imported from India and Nepal, camping gear and

military surplus equipment are regular items. The best bargains are household goods such as pots and pans, dishes, drinking glasses and second-hand books.

You might feel overwhelmed by the scale of the market, the bustling crowds and the heat, but take time to wander because this is the ideal place to buy Thai handicrafts or souvenirs. Be sure to bargain good-naturedly, pitching your initial offer at least 50 per cent below the asking price.

One unfortunate aspect of the market is the sale of some endangered wildlife, both living (as pets) and dead (for medicine or the cooking pot). Recently the Thai authorities have moved to crack down on this illicit trade, which is far less prevalent than it was a decade or so ago.

Plenty of interesting and tasty food and drink stalls, and live music towards the end of the day, complete the recommended full-day visit. Although the market is mainly open on weekends, a few vendors are out on weekday mornings and there is a daily vegetable, plant and flower market opposite the weekend market's south side.

✠ *Bangkok 7f* (off map) ✉ Southern end of Chatuchak Park, off Thanon Phahon Yothin, Bangkok 🕔 Sat–Sun 8–6 ✋ Free 🍴 Cafés throughout the market 🚇 Chatuchak 🚉 N8, Mor Chit Station ❓ Music in the late afternoon

2 Doi Inthanon

www.dnp.go.th

Thailand's highest peak hosts a unique ecosystem of sub-Himalayan flora and fauna.

Encompassed in a 428sq km (167sq-mile) national park, the 2,595m-high (8512ft) Doi Inthanon was named after Phra Inthawichayanon, the last ruler of Chiang Mai, who died at the turn of the 19th century. His remains lie interred in a small white *chedi* (pagoda) near the summit. Long celebrated by the people of the north for its natural beauty and cool climate, the mountain has much to offer, including unspoiled hill-tribe villages, several striking waterfalls and dramatic mountain scenery.

Once the habitat of bears and tigers, the park has seen the severe depletion of its wildlife by overhunting and increased human settlement. Nevertheless, it is still possible to see rare mammals such as flying squirrels, red-toothed shrews, Chinese pangolins and Père David's vole, as well as a plethora of birds, butterflies and moths. Rainfall on the slopes is high, with frequent showers even during the dry season. This encourages myriad varieties of ferns, mosses and orchids to flourish, often completely covering the trunks of even the tallest trees.

Nearer the summit stand two tall pagodas built to honour the Thai king and

queen. These remarkable structures, set amid carefully tended gardens of temperate flowers and vegetables, are among the most architecturally innovative buildings of their kind in Thailand. Particularly noteworthy are the modernistic interpretations of traditional Buddhist themes portrayed in copper-coloured tiles on the face of the king's *chedi*. In borders nearby, fuchsias, petunias, hydrangeas, helichrysums and salvias blend unexpectedly with decorative cabbages, adding to the location's charm.

✚ 6B ✉ 113km (70 miles) southwest of Chiang Mai 🕙 Daily ✋ Expensive 🍴 Cafés next to royal *chedis* and at the summit 🚌 Buses from Chiang Mai to Chom Thong, then *songthaews* (pick-up vans converted to buses) to summit

ℹ Chiang Mai–Lamphun Road, Chiang Mai ☎ 053 248 604

3 Grand Palace

www.palaces.thai.net

A wealth of cultural and architectural delights awaits visitors here.

The greatest site in Bangkok and a definite 'must' on any itinerary is the Grand Palace and the surrounding monuments on Ratanakosin Island, the water-enclosed old city of Bangkok.

This city within a city forms an enormous 24ha (59-acre) walled complex. Within it, more than 100 mansions, halls, pavilions and temples with exquisite mosaic-encrusted spires and pillars make up a fascinating combination of Victorian, Italian Renaissance and other styles, the oldest of which dates back 200 years. Beautiful murals found inside the compound walls show the Ramakien, the Thai version of the Hindu epic, the Ramayana. Lovingly restored, they date from King Rama I (1782–1809).

The palace itself is only used by the monarch on certain ceremonial occasions; his official residence in Bangkok is Dusit Palace. The main attraction is Wat Phra Kaeo, the 'Temple of the Emerald Buddha'. This tiny but elegant Buddha image, made of jasper and not emerald, is only 75cm (29in) high and stands at the heart of the temple on a high pedestal encased in glass. Regarded as the Palladium of the Kingdom, it cannot be photographed and – perhaps partly because of this

– it is surrounded by an almost palpable aura of mystery and respect.

In a row on the northern side of the temple are the Phra Si Ratana, a golden *chedi*; Phra Mondop, containing a Buddhist library not open to the public; and Prasad Phra Thep Bidom, the royal pantheon.

✚ *Bangkok 2d* ✉ Thanon Sanam Cha
☎ 026 235 499 ⏰ Daily 8.30–3.30
✋ Expensive 🚌 8, 12

4 Khao Sok National Park

www.khaosok.com

This 650sq km (253 sq-mile) park in Surat Thani, southern Thailand, boasts original rainforest with waterfalls, limestone cliffs and an island-studded lake.

Established in 1980, Khao Sok connects with two other national parks, Kaeng Krung and Phang-nga, along with the Khlong Saen and Khlong Nakha wildlife sanctuaries. Together, they form the largest contiguous nature preserve in peninsular Thailand.

Home to elephants, leopards, serow (antelope), gaur (wild Indian cattle), langur monkeys, banteng (wild oxen) and Malayan sun bears, as well as almost 200 bird species, the park also shelters tigers, seriously threatened elsewhere in Thailand by poachers (the Khao Sok tiger population itself is thought to number less than 10).

Flora includes lianas, bamboo, rattan, ferns and the spectacular *Raffelesia*, the giant lotus – its flower reaches 80cm (31in) in diameter and is the

largest in the world. The plant has no roots or leaves of its own; instead it lives parasitically inside the roots of the liana. When the bud blooms in January it emits a powerful scent which attracts pollinating insects.

The best time of year to visit Khao Sok is in the dry season (December to May), when trails are less slippery, river crossings are easier and riverbank camping is considered safe. However, during the wet season, sightings of larger animals such as bear, civet, deer, elephant, slow loris, wild boar, gaur and even tiger are more likely. During dry months the larger animals tend to stay near the reservoir in areas without trails.

The park headquarters and guest houses near the park entrance can arrange guided hikes to the main waterfalls and caves. Leeches are quite common in certain areas of the park, so take sensible precautions – wear closed shoes when hiking and apply copious insect repellent.

✚ 13P ✉ Off Route 401, 100km (62 miles) north of Phuket
🕐 Daily 💰 Expensive 🍴 Restaurants at resorts just outside the park 🚌 Bus from Phuket to Takua Pa, bus from Takua Pa to Surat Thani, get off at KM 109

5 Mekong River

One of the world's great waterways, the Mekong flows for more than 4,500km (2,790 miles) – a third of which meanders between Thailand and Laos.

Until recently the Mekong formed part of the 'bamboo curtain' between communist and non-communist Asia. It is now fast becoming a gateway to Laos and Cambodia, as well as a fascinating crossroads for Indo-Chinese culture.

Rising in a distant region of China, the Mekong passes through six countries before emptying into the South China Sea. For 1,500km (930 miles) of this course, the mighty river flows partly in Thai territory, first appearing at Sop Ruak in the far north and forming the border between Thailand and Laos as far as Chiang Kham (town of the giant Mekong catfish or *plaa beuk*) before cutting back into Laos. It reappears in Thailand near Chiang Khan in Isaan, Thailand's northeastern region, and again forms the Thai–Lao border in a great arc, finally disappearing into Laos just beyond Khong Jiam on its way to the thunderous Khone Falls.

The Mekong is Isaan's lifeline, a constant source of water. As a consequence, the riverside settlements which border it from Chiang Khan in the north to Mukdahan and beyond in the east are the most favoured parts of Isaan – and the most interesting towns to visit.

The Mekong can be experienced in the north at Chiang Saen and the Golden Triangle (➤ 156), or during the long and relaxing drive from Chiang Khan to Nong Khai and even on to Mukdahan.

✚ 9C–12F ✉ The border in north and northeast Thailand 🍴 Restaurants the complete length 🚌 Regular air-conditioned buses to all major towns on the river from Bangkok 🚆 Train to Nong Khai 🚤 Boats from Chiang Saen to Sop Ruak and from Chiang Khong to Luang Prabang, Laos

6 Ao Phang-nga

About 95km (59 miles) from Phuket, the area around Ao Phang-nga (Phang-nga Bay) is startlingly beautiful – sheer limestone cliffs ring the bay, while unlikely karst towers, carved over the millennia into extraordinary shapes, rise sheer from the azure waters.

The bay can be explored aboard large boats on organized tours, or individually chartered 'long-tail' boats that are fast but noisy. Nothing beats kayaking in the region, however. The inflatable kayaks or canoes can enter semi-submerged caves inaccessible to larger boats, sometimes passing beneath overhangs so low that the canoeist has to lie flat.

Absolute silence reigns within these sea caves, save for the dripping of water from a nearby stalactite or the splash of a paddle. One visitor noted that he was startled by the beating of a butterfly's wings. The caves often open into large hidden bowls, inaccessible from the top, which fill with sunlight during the day and are home to interesting flora and fauna, including flocks of swallows, the nests of which are used to make bird's-nest soup.

Other sights to look for when exploring Ao Phang-nga are 'James Bond Island', a narrow island tower made famous in the 007 movie *The Man With the Golden Gun*, and the Muslim fishing village on Panyi Island.

✚ 13Q ✉ Ao Phang-nga, 788km (489 miles) south of Bangkok, 95km (59 miles) north of Phuket 🚌 Regular air-conditioned buses from Bangkok and Phuket 🛥 Boat trips into Ao Phang-nga from Tha Dan ✈ Phuket Airport ❓ Sea Canoe Thailand ☎ 076 212 172; www.seacanoe.net ✋ Moderate
ℹ 73–75 Thanon Phuket, Phuket ☎ 076 212 213

7 Prasat Phanom Rung

Built between the 10th and 13th centuries, Prasat Phanom Rung is the largest and best preserved Khmer monument outside Cambodia.

The architecture of the kingdom of Angkor reached its height during the reign of King Suriyavarman II (AD1113–50), when the greater part of the work on Prasat Phanom Rung was completed.

Phanom Rung was originally built as a Hindu temple honouring the deities Vishnu and Shiva.

Beautifully carved representations of these two gods adorn the lintels and pediments of the sanctuary, together with figures of Nandi, the bull mount of Shiva and Uma. On the east portico of the antechamber is a fine *nataraja* or dancing Shiva figure. Beyond, in the rust-coloured central section of the sanctuary, is a pillar-like Shiva *lingam* (phallic image).

The Phra Narai lintel, a carved relief bearing the image of Lord Narayana (a manifestation of Vishnu), is over the east-facing front entrance. Growing from his navel is a lotus blossom, on a branch of which sits Brahma, the Hindu lord of creation.

One of the most impressive sights of the sanctuary is from the west-facing promenade that leads to the main temple. In the early morning, the rising sun illuminates *naga* (mythical Hindu water serpent) balustrades and the steps which lead to the inner complex containing the central *mondop* (ante-chamber) and main *prang* (spire). To the right of the promenade is the White Elephant Hall.

The climb to the sanctuary from the car park is gradual and passes a number of small museum buildings housing artefacts from the site, including carved stone lintels. It took 20 years to restore the sanctuary.

🚩 18G 📧 144km (89 miles) southeast of Nakhon Ratchasima 🕐 Daily 6–6 💷 Inexpensive 🍴 Food stalls at entrance 🚌 Regular buses from Nakhon Ratchasima, Buriram and Surin ❓ Phanom Rung Festival, Mar
ℹ Mittaphap Road, Nakhon Ratchasima ☎ 044 213 666

⑧ Similan Islands

The Similans are renowned for their rich coral reefs, clear waters and pristine beaches. These islands are a naturalist's paradise.

Marine animals include whale sharks, manta rays, bottlenose dolphins and large pelagic fish, along with interesting smaller life from garden eels to feather stars. More than 30 species of resident birds, such as the white-breasted waterhen and Brahminy kite, and migratory species, including the cattle egret, pintail snipe, grey wagtail and roseate tern, occupy the islands. Small mammals include the bush-tailed porcupine, common palm civet and flying lemur. Reptiles and amphibians include the banded krait, reticulated python, white-lipped pit viper, common pit viper, hawksbill turtle, leatherback turtle, Bengal monitor lizard and common water monitor lizard.

The name 'Similan' derives from the Malay word *sembilan* or nine and refers to the nine islands in the group. All are relatively small and uninhabited except for park officials and tour groups.

Divers generally prefer visiting the Similans on one of the many live-aboard boats that operate out of Phuket. Other visitors stay on Ko Miang, second in size to Ko Similan, where there is a visitor centre, the park headquarters and the archipelago's only land accommodation. The beaches on this island are especially good for shallow-water snorkelling. Nearby Ko Similan is popular for walking and snorkelling. The largest granite outcrop in the archipelago is also found on Ko Similan and from the top there is a fine view of the surrounding sea.

Boats run to the Similans between November and May. The best diving months are between December and May; for the rest of the year, the seas are too rough and water visibility is reduced.

➕ 13P ✉ 100km (62 miles) northwest of Phuket
🕐 All year round 🍴 Restaurant on Ko Miang
💷 Expensive 🚢 Regular tour boats from Phuket
ℹ 73–75 Thanon Phuket, Phuket ☎ 076 212 213

Sukhothai Historical Park

www.su.ac.th/sukhothai

The remains of 21 structures lie within the old walls of the capital of the first Thai kingdom, once fortified by three ramparts and two moats.

Ramkhamhaeng National Museum provides a good starting point for an exploration of the ruins. A replica of the famous Ramkhamhaeng inscription – the earliest known example of Thai script, dating from the reign of King Ramkhamhaeng of Sukhothai (1279–98) – is on display, together with a fine collection of Sukhothai artefacts.

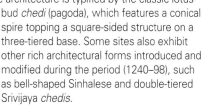

Sukhothai temple architecture is typified by the classic lotus-bud *chedi* (pagoda), which features a conical spire topping a square-sided structure on a three-tiered base. Some sites also exhibit other rich architectural forms introduced and modified during the period (1240–98), such as bell-shaped Sinhalese and double-tiered Srivijaya *chedis*.

The spiritual and administrative centre of the old capital, Wat Mahathat is the largest temple in the city and dates from the 13th century. Surrounded by brick walls and a moat, the *chedi* exhibits the lotus-bud motif while almost 200 original Buddha images survive among the ruined columns. Just to the south, the 12th-century Wat Si Sawai, originally a Hindu temple, features three Khmer-style *prangs* (spires) and a picturesque moat.

Next to the museum, Wat Trapang Thong is a small, still functioning temple with fine

stucco reliefs. It is reached by a footbridge across the large lotus-filled pond surrounding it. This tank, which still supplies the Sukhothai community with most of its water, is supposedly the original site of Thailand's Loy Krathong Festival (when lighted candles are set adrift on rivers and canals in honour of Mae Kongka, goddess of the waterways).

The elephant, an animal traditionally held in great esteem by the Thais, features prominently at Sukhothai. Wat Chang Lom (Elephant Circled Monastery) is about 1km (0.5 miles) east of the main park entrance. A large bell-shaped *chedi* is supported by 36 elephants sculpted into its base. On another hill west of the city, just south of Wat Saphaan Hin, Wat Chang Rop features another elephant-based *chedi*.

✚ 7D ✉ Old Sukhothai, 12km (7 miles) from New Sukhothai; 400km (248 miles) north of Bangkok ③ Daily 8.30–5 ✋ Inexpensive 🍴 Food stalls within the park 🚌 Regular *songthaews* from New Sukhothai ✈ Sukhothai Airport ❓ Loy Krathong Festival, Nov ℹ Sukhothai Information Office ☎ 055 697 310

10 Wat Phra That Lampang Luang

Believed to contain a genuine Buddha relic, northern Thailand's most beautiful temple is revered by the Thai people.

Established in Mon times, during the Kingdom of Haripunchai, Wat Phra That Lampang Luang

(the Great Temple of Lampang) is in Ko Kha district, 18km (11 miles) southwest of the city of Lampang. It was originally a *wiang* or fortified temple protected by massive earthen ramparts. The tall central *chedi* (pagoda) is believed to contain a bone fragment of the Buddha and is widely revered by Thai people, especially the Khon Muang (northern Thais).

On important religious holidays, notably at Songkran (Thai New Year) and Loy Krathong (Festival of Lights) each November full moon, the temple attracts huge crowds of devout worshippers from Lampang and more distant provinces. Particularly venerated is the Phra Kaeo Don Tao, a jasper Buddha image believed to have mystical powers.

In architectural terms, Wat Phra That Lampang Luang is one of Thailand's most elegant temples. The central *viharn* (chapel), featuring a triple-tiered wooden roof supported by massive teak pillars, is thought to be the oldest wooden building in Thailand. Early 19th-century murals from the Buddhist *jatakas* or life stories are painted on wooden panels within the *viharn*. The lintel (horizontal support) over the main entrance to the compound has an impressive intertwined dragon relief – once common in northern Thai temples but rarely seen today.

✚ 7C ✉ 18km (11 miles) southwest of Lampang city (which is 90km/59 miles southeast of Chiang Mai), Ko Kha district, north Thailand ⏰ Daily 6–6 ✋ Free 🍴 Food stalls outside temple complex 🚌 Regular *songthaews* from Lampang 🚆 Lampang Station ✈ Lampang Airport

Best things to do

Good places to have lunch

Border View (BB)

Thai, Chinese and Western food is presented on a beautiful terrace overlooking the Mekong River. True to its name, there are magnificent views of the mythical Golden Triangle area.

✉ 222 Golden Triangle, Sop Ruak ☎ 053 784 001–5 🕔 Lunch, dinner

Bussaracum (BBB)

Enjoy royal Thai cuisine (recipes created for the Thai royal court), exquisitely presented in this elegant restaurant

✉ 139 Sethiwan Building, Thanon Pun, Bangkok ☎ 022 666 312 🕔 Lunch, dinner 🚌 530 🚇 Surasuk Station

Captain's Choice (BBB)

One of Ko Samui's top restaurants, and renowned for its seafood. Ask for a table on the beach for a really atmospheric experience.

✉ Choeng Mon Beach, Ko Samui ☎ 077 425 041 🕔 Lunch, dinner

Indochine (BB)

This is one of Thailand's best Vietnamese restaurants, located in an old teak house. Try the cha gio (spring rolls), nem nuong (spicy pork meatballs) and pho (beef noodle soup).

✉ Wat Jaeng, Thanon Samphasit, Ubon Ratchathani ☎ 045 245 584 🕔 Breakfast, lunch, early evening

Le Coq d'Or (BBB)

Originally British consul's residence and now Chiang Mai's top French restaurant. Excellent food and wine.

✉ 11 Soi 2 Thanon Ko Klang, Chiang Mai ☎ 053 282 024 🕔 Lunch, dinner

Lemongrass (BB)

Central Thai food (such as southern-style weet and spicy grilled chicken) served in an elegant old wooden house. Book ahead.

✉ 5/1 Soi 24 Thanon Sukhumvit, Bangkok ☎ 022 588 637 🕔 Lunch, dinner 🚌 501, 508, 511 🚇 E5 Phrom Phong Station

Lobster Pot (BBB)

Much more than just lobsters are on the menu at the Lobster Pot. On a pier over Pattaya Bay, this fine restaurant serves the best seafood in town – all at a price of course.

✉ 288 Beach Road, Pattaya ☎ 038 426 083 🕒 Lunch, dinner

Riverside (BB)

Enjoy good Thai and European food combined with a friendly atmosphere and wonderful views of the river. There is also a popular bar and live music most nights.

✉ 9/11 Thanon Charoen Rat, Chiang Mai ☎ 053 243 239 🕒 Lunch, dinner

Tropica (BB)

Italian food and good wines served in a beautiful tropical garden.

✉ Beach Road, Patong Beach, Pattaya ☎ 076 341 193; www.tropica-bungalow.com 🕒 Breakfast, lunch, dinner

Ways to be a local

Drink Thai whisky in a local bar Local brands (the most popular is Mekong) are cheaper even than beer. Ask for it with soda and fresh lemon for a refreshing version.

Go to a temple Make an offering of incense or flowers as Thai people often do, although do dress respectfully and remove your shoes.

Thai cooking Learn how to find your way around a Thai market and create delicious, delicately spiced dishes. Chiang Mai (► 148–153) is home to a number of cookery schools, and the best place to improve your culinary skills.

Visit a market and bargain hard This can cut the prices of goods by more than half, even in shopping centres.

Thai massage Learn how to give a traditional Thai treatment at Wat Pho in Bangkok – the national headquarters for Thai massage.
✉ 2 Sanamchai Road, Bangkok, 10200
☎ 022 211 969; www.watpho.com

Take a *tuk-tuk* These three-wheeled vehicles are much more fun than a traditional taxi and much faster in heavy traffic.

Make a boat trip Chug down the Chao Phraya River in a traditional long-tail boat and catch a glimpse of everyday city life in Bangkok.

Go to a language school Or, if it seems too daunting to learn the language, at least learn how to make a Thai greeting. People in Thailand do not shake hands, they 'wai' – a gesture made by placing their hands together in front of their face and bowing a little.

Attend a boxing match *Muay Thai* (Thai boxing) is the national sport and while combative, it has an undeniable spiritual dimension. Matches take place throughout the country and at **Lumpini Stadium** (➤ 121) in Bangkok throughout the week.

Visit the Loy Krathong Festival (➤ 25)
All over the country, during the November full moon period, tribute is made to the Goddess of Rivers with a beautiful display of small boats with flowers and candles.

Out and about

Bird-watching Nearly 1,000 species of birds live in Thailand. It is possible to spot tropical birds by the Mekong River (➤ 44–45), in the mountainous north, or by lagoons in the south.

Cycling Outside Bangkok, bikes are a great way to travel around Thailand and can be rented in most locations. The large historical sites, such as Sukhothai and Ayutthaya, particularly lend themselves to visits on two wheels.

Dancing Get down at world-class discos in Bangkok, Phuket, Ko Samui and Chiang Mai (➤ 120–121, 145, 171).

Elephant Nature Park Learn about these incredible creatures at this elephant sanctuary north of Chiang Mai, rather than taking a touristy ride. A day tour includes feeding and swimming with the animals, which must be booked in advance.
☎ 053 272 855; www.elephantnaturepark.org

Golf The country has more than 200 highly rated golf courses nationwide. There are at least a few courses in or within easy reach of all major cities, such as Bangkok's Kan Tarat Golf Course, which sits among the runways of Don Muang Airport (➤ 26).

Fishing Try your luck at landing a big catch from Mekong River (➤ 44–45) or off the long coastline. Phuket is a particularly good option, as an island destination that also has a freshwater lake (➤ 124–127).

Shopping Indulge yourself in some retail therapy in the markets and malls of Bangkok (➤ 116–120) and Chiang Mai (➤ 170–171). Antiques, silks, clothes and textiles are all good buys.

Sunbathing Thailand has some of the world's best beaches. The large open stretches of fine sand on Ko Samui (➤ 131) and Phuket (➤ 124–127) are very popular, while Hat Sai Daeng on the tiny island of Ko Tao (➤ 132) is a more intimate alternative.

Swimming Thailand's warm, clear seas invite swimmers. Smaller islands such as Ko Pha-Ngan (➤ 131) and Phi Phi (➤ 126), with their calm, quiet waters, are particularly good bets.

Walking Take to the hills of Northern Thailand on a several-day trek, or for a more gentle stroll, follow signposted trails in many of the country's national parks, such as Doi Inthanon (➤ 38–39).

Great adventures

Caving Thailand has some spectacular cave systems, such as those around Chiang Mai (➤ 148–149) and Mae Hong Son (➤ 157); some of the largest on earth.

Diving The Similan Islands (➤ 50–51) are one of the top diving destinations in the world. The Sea Dragon Dive Center runs a variety of trips.
Sea Dragon Dive Centre ✉ 9/1 Mu 7, T. Khuk Khak, Khao Lak, A. Takua Pa, Phang Nga 82190 ☎ 076 420 420; www.seadragondivecenter.com

Horse-back riding Thailand's scenery creates a stunning backdrop for rides. The Phuket Bangtao (Laguna) Riding Club takes you through jungles, plantations and onto beautiful beaches.
Phuket Bangtao Riding Club ✉ Entrance to Laguna Bang Tao, T. Cherng Talay, A. Thalang, Phuket 83110 ☎ 076 324 199; www.phuket-bangtao-horseriding.com

Mountain biking Thailand's hilly north is ideal for mountain biking: Pai has forest cycle trails and there are scenic routes around Chiang Mai (➤ 148–149).

Parasailing This sport is possible at many of the more commercial beaches, such as Phuket (➤ 124–127) and Pattaya (➤ 105).

Rock climbing The magnificent coastal cliffs near the town of Krabi (➤ 132) in the south of Thailand are a magnet for climbers, as are the country's limestone mountains. Contact the Thailand Rock Climbing Federation for further information.
Thailand Rock Climbing Federation ☎ 023 738 725

Sailing The waters around Phuket, dotted with the unusual islands and caves of Ao Phang-nga (➤ 46–47), make for interesting sailing. YachtPro offers both courses and charters in this region.
YachtPro ✉ 183/53 Phang Nga Road, Phuket
☎ 076 232 960

Sea canoeing Explore the sea caves and karst towers of Ao Phang-nga (➤ 46–47) or witness the scenery of Krabi (➤ 132) or Phuket (➤ 124–127) with the chance to see local wildlife on a boat trip.

Trekking The lush mountains in the north provide a beautiful backdrop to trekking trips, as does the peak of Khao Luang in the national park of the same name in the south.

White-water rafting Most travel agencies in Chiang Mai and Chiang Rai offer white-water rafting and canoeing expeditions in remote areas of northern Thailand. The Peak arranges adventure tours and rafting trips on the Maetang River, 60km (36 miles) north of Chiang Mai.
The Peak Adventure Tour ✉ Thanon Changklan (behind the Night Bazaar), Chiang Mai ☎ 053 800 567–8; www.thepeakadventure.com

Stunning views

Best shopping

Ban Boran Textiles
Showcases gorgeous fabrics from six countries in Southeast Asia. The fabrics are made into shirts, trousers, skirts and dresses.
✉ 51 Thanon Yaowarat, Phuket ☎ 076 212 473

Big C
This chain of shopping complexes selling mostly food and household goods can be found throughout the country from Chiang Rai in the north to Hat Yai in the south (➤ 187).

Chatuchak Weekend Market
See pages 36–37.

Gaysorn Plaza
This shopping centre has excellent household accessories shops, with contemporary Thai-style items.
✉ Corner of Thanon Ratchadamri and Ploenchit 🚇 Chidlom Station, Bangkok
🚌 504, 505, 514

Gemopolis
This gem centre is supported by the Thai Government so you can be pretty sure you are buying the real deal. Everything is tax free.
✉ Gemopolis Industrial Estate, 47/31 Moo 4 Thanon Sukhapiban 2, Bangkok
☎ 027 270 204–5; www.gemopolis.com 🚌 12, 44

Hang Dong
This village just south of Chiang Mai is the main centre in the area for woodcarvings and rattan furniture.
✉ Hang Dong, Route 108, near Chiang Mai

Jim Thompson Silk Shop
This is perhaps the best place for silk in Bangkok, with high-quality clothing and household accessories.
✉ 9 Thanon Surawong, Bangkok ☎ 022 344 900 🚌 112, 502, 504

Night Bazaar

This night bazaar is a shopping haven full of fake perfumes, designer copies and tourist junk, as well as lacquerware, woodcarvings, silverwork, antiques and spices (➤ 153).

✉ Thanon Chang Khlan, Chiang Mai

Siam Paragon

One of Asia's largest department stores has an overwhelming selection of goods from fashion to cars. And if you tire of shopping, you can take in a film at one of the cinemas, or zone out at the basement aquarium.

✉ Siam Square, Bangkok 🚌 73, 79, 204 🚇 Siam Station

World Trade Centre

An enormous shopping centre with everything from high-end boutiques to the best music shops in Bangkok. It also houses the very chic Zen Department Store and an ice-skating rink.

✉ Junction of Thanon Ratchadamri and Thanon Rama I 🚌 504, 505, 514
🚇 E1 Chidlom Station, Bangkok

Places to take the children

Ancient City

This huge park faithfully reproduces scaled-down versions of Thailand's most famous sights. Children will also love the nearby Samut Park crocodile farm and zoo.

✉ Old Sukhumvit Highway, Bangpu, Samut Prakan, Bangkok ☎ 023 239 253; www.ancientcity.com 🕐 Daily 8–5 🚌 7, 8, 11 (Samut Prakan terminal, then minibus 36)

Aquarium and Marine Biological Research Centre

Hundreds of tropical fish and other marine species found mostly in local waters are exhibited in this beautifully situated aquarium.

✉ Route 4129, at the tip of Phanwa Cape (10km/6 miles from Phuket Town) ☎ 076 391 125; www.pmbc.go.th 🕐 Daily 8.30–4

Chiang Mai Zoo

A beautiful zoo 6km (4 miles) from the middle of town at the foot of the Doi Suthep mountain. You can drive a vehicle around the zoo, but if you are walking be warned that it is particularly hilly.

✉ Thanon Huay Kaew, Chiaing Mai 🕐 Daily 8–5

Dream World Amusement Park

Amusement park on a grand scale, with rides and shows, including Snowland, Uncle Tom's Farm and the Magic Cabaret Show.

✉ KM7, Rangsit–Nakhon Nayok Highway (Klong 3), Bangkok ☎ 025 331 152; www.dreamworld-th.com 🕐 Mon–Fri 10–5, Sat–Sun 10–7 🚌 21, 95

Fantasea

A large cultural theme park that explores Thailand's 'Myths,

Mysteries and Magic'. Open in the evenings.

✉ 99 Moo 3 Kamala Beach, Phuket ☎ 076 385 000 🕓 Fri–Wed 5–11pm

Pattaya Kart Speedway

With a circuit at slightly over a kilometre (0.5 miles) long, this is a fun place to spend an afternoon. Different powered vehicles for adults and children.

✉ 248/2 Thanon Thepprasit, Pattaya ☎ 038 422 044 🕓 Daily 9.30–6.30

Phuket Butterfly Garden and Aquarium

Spread over 2,800sq m (3,350sq yd), the three main areas are Butterfly Garden, Marine World and Insect Room.

✉ 71/6 Moo 5 Soi Panaeng, Yaowarat Road, Phuket ☎ 076 215 616
🕓 Daily 9–5.30

Phuket Seashell Museum

One of the world's most valuable collections of seashells on display. Numerous rarities and freaks including the world's largest golden pearl and a shell weighing 250kg (550lb).

✉ Rawai Beach, Phuket ☎ 076 381 266/74 🕓 Daily 8–7

Safari World

Billed as the largest open zoo in the world, Safari World is divided into two parts – the 5km (3-mile) Safari Park drive featuring various land animals and the Marine Park, exhibiting marine and rare animals.

✉ 99 Ramindra 1, Minburi, Bangkok ☎ 025 181 000 🕓 Mon–Fri 9–5.30,
Sat–Sun 9–9

Sainumphung Orchid and Butterfly Farm

Lots of beautiful orchids to see and buy and a butterfly farm where children learn about the life of a butterfly.

✉ 60–61 Moo 1, Rim Tai, Mae Rim, Chiang Mai ☎ 053 297 892
🕓 Daily 7–5

Best beaches

Ao Loh Dalum
Ko Phi Phi's (➤ 126) main beach can get crowded, but it is a lovely crescent of sand flanked by emerald waters and lush vegetation.

Chaweng
Ko Samui's (➤ 131) principal beach on the eastern side of the island, lined with restaurants, hotels and bars, has a distinctly cosmopolitan atmosphere.

Hua Hin
Thailand's oldest resort is also a royal retreat. Although the 5km (3-mile) beach is not the prettiest in the country, it is nonetheless charming, with its old-fashioned parasols, striped deckchairs and horse rides on the sand (➤ 128).

Hat Rai Leh
Spectacular limestone cliffs fringe the coast here, near the town of Krabi (➤ 132), which is studded with craggy islands.

Hat Rin Nok
The small, pretty 'Sunrise Beach' on the island of Ko Pha-Ngan (➤ 131) tends to attract a younger crowd, who come to enjoy the hedonistic New Moon parties and simple accommodation.

Hat Sai Kaew
'Diamond Beach' on Ko Samet (➤ 104) is, true to its name, a sparkling white expanse. It is a lovely spot to sunbathe or shop by day, and tuck into some local seafood at night, entertained by fire-eaters on the sand.

Hat Sai Khao
'White Sand Beach' on the island of Ko Chang (➤ 104) forms a long stretch of sand backed by lush green trees and still manages to retain a rustic feel.

Hat Sai Ree
This almost idyllic beach on the tiny, turtle-shaped island of Ko Tao (➤ 132) appeals to divers and those who really want to get away from it all.

Jomtien
This is one of the more attractive beaches near the large international resort of Pattaya (➤ 105), with a range of watersports available.

Patong
By day Patong, on the popular island of Phuket, offers almost every kind of water sport imaginable; when night falls its discos and bars come into their own (➤ 126).

Top Thai dishes

Gaeng Kheow Wan Gai (green chicken curry)
Green chillies, kaffir lime leaves and lemongrass, and coconut milk are just some of the ingredients of this hot sauce, which is served with chicken and Thai aubergine (eggplant).

Gai Pad Met Ma-muang Himmaphan (chicken fried with cashew nuts)
This robust dish, which sometimes includes vegetables, has a thick glaze of fish and oyster sauce.

Nuea Satay (beef satay)
Beef marinated in coconut milk, curry powder and fish sauce and pan fried is traditionally served on long skewers with a small dish of rich peanut sauce.

Pad Ka Pao (meat fried with sweet basil)
Delicious sweet basil (a sweet version of normal basil), baby sweet corn and fried pork are used in this dish, which is usually served with fluffy rice.

Pad Thai (Thai fried noodles)
A street-stall favourite that can be bought cheaply throughout Thailand. Shallots are pounded with palm sugar and garlic and mixed with an unusual combination of peanuts, dried shrimp, bean sprouts and scrambled eggs.

Phanaeng Nuea (stir-fry beef curry)
Beef (which can be replaced with chicken) is covered in a rich sauce of coconut, curry and peppers.

Som Tam (papaya salad)
An unusual, spicy salad of shredded, firm, dark green papaya, chillies, garlic, anchovy sauce and green beans.

Tom Kha Gai (chicken in coconut soup)
A rich, aromatic soup made with fresh kaffir lime leaves, young galangal, chicken and coconut milk.

Yam Nuea (spicy beef salad)
This dish is very popular in both Thai homes and in restaurants. Tender barbecued beef steak is thinly sliced and tossed in a salad of onions, tomato, cucumber and peppers, with a dressing of lime juice, garlic and fish sauce.

Tom Yum Kung (spicy shrimp soup)
This is a wonderful, richly flavoured soup of juicy prawns, galangal (a little like fresh ginger), mushrooms, lemongrass and chilli.

a walk

around the island of Ko Ratanakosin

This walk encompasses the central part of historic Bangkok, known to the Thais as Ko Ratanakosin (Ratanakosin Island) because it is isolated from the rest of the city by a network of canals connecting with the Chao Phraya River.

Begin your walk at the Lak Muang, or city pillar, traditionally regarded as the heart of the city. Situated at the intersection of Thanon Ratchadamnoen Nai and Thanon Lak Muang, this shrine is best reached by taxi.

From Lak Muang walk south with the Grand Palace walls to your right. Turn right along Thanon Chetuphon and after about 500m (545yds) you will reach the impressive entrance to Wat Pho.

Officially known as Wat Phra Chetuphon, this is Bangkok's oldest and grandest temple, with a spectacular reclining Buddha. It is also renowned for its massage school, and visitors can enjoy a relaxing and invigorating traditional massage at a very reasonable price.

After leaving Wat Pho head north along Thanon Maharat beside the river to Tha Tien pier. Here catch a cross-river ferry to Wat Arun on the far bank.

Wat Arun or the 'Temple of Dawn' has a striking, Khmer-style *prang* or spire, virtually the whole of which is decorated with shards of porcelain. The steps are steep and narrow – avoid the climb if you suffer from vertigo.

From Wat Arun cross by ferry back to Ratanakosin Island and continue north along Maharat Road. Near Tha Chang pier turn right onto Thanon Na Phra Lan. Enter the Grand Palace's main entrance.

The Grand Palace and its temple, Wat Phra Kaeo, are outstanding examples of early Ratanakosin architecture. You are free to wander about, but dress respectfully and do not photograph the Emerald Buddha.

Distance 2.5km (1.5 miles)
Time 2–4 hours, depending on temple visits
Start point Lak Muang, Thanon Ratchadamnoen Nai ✚ *Bangkok 2d*
🚌 7, 9, 11 **End point** The Grand Palace ✚ *Bangkok 2d*
Lunch Lan Theh (£) ✉ Tha Maharat Pier, Chao Phraya River

National parks

Top museums

Bangkok National Museum

This Bangkok treasure trove is the biggest museum in Southeast Asia and holds a fine collection of ceramics, textiles, woodcarvings, weaponry and traditional musical instruments. If you only go to one museum, make it this one. Its royal family memorabilia and historical artefacts are among the finest in Southeast Asia (➤ 93).

✉ Thanon Na Phra That, Bangkok ☎ 022 241 370 🕐 Wed–Sun 9–4 💰 Inexpensive 🚌 7, 9, 11, 39

Chao Sam Phraya National Museum

This museum is crammed full of of gold treasures, including an elephant adorned in jewels. It also houses a large selection of Ayutthayan period Buddhist sculpture.

✉ Thanon Rotchana, Ayutthaya 🕐 Wed–Sun 9–4 💰 Inexpensive

Chiang Mai National Museum

A fine collection of Buddha images in a variety of styles.

✉ Superhighway 11, near Wat Jet Yot 🕐 Wed–Sun 9–4 💰 Inexpensive

Hill Tribe Museum

Handicrafts, jewellery, costumes and other items used by Thailand's hill people form the well-presented displays here. Information is given about the various communities, each with their distinctive beliefs, dress and farming methods.

✉ Ratchamangkhala Park, north of Chiang Mai 🕐 Mon–Fri 9–4 💰 Free

Jim Thompson's House

A collection of Southeast Asian art in a traditional Thai residence once owned by an American entrepreneur (➤ 93).

✉ 6 Soi Kasemsan 2, off Thanon Rama 1, Bangkok ☎ 022 167 368 🕐 Daily 9–5 💰 Moderate 🚇 Center Siam Station 🚌 1, 2, 8

Hall of Opium

This excellent museum, situated in a small valley above the Mekong, is one of two in the Sop Ruak area dedicated to opium. Visitors are taken on a journey through tunnels filled with strange music and the simulated scent of opium before entering rooms explaining the fascinating history of the drug.

 Moo 1 Ban Sop Ruak, Tambon Wiang, Amphoe Chiang Saen (10km/6 miles northwest of Chiang Saen) ☎ 053 784 444–5 🕐 Thu–Sun 8.30–4 ✋ Expensive

Ramkhamhaeng National Museum

An excellent collection of Sukhothai-period objects; probably the best place to start a visit to the ruins in this area (➤ 52).

✉ Sukhothai Historical Park 🕐 Daily 9–4 ✋ Inexpensive

Royal Barges National Museum

A collection of the king's ceremonial boats and barges, used each year at the end of the Buddhist Rains Retreat.

✉ Bangkok Noi Canal, Thonburi side of Chao Phraya River ☎ 024 240 004 🕐 Daily 9–5. Closed 31 Dec, 1 Jan, 12–14 Apr ✋ Inexpensive 🚌 7, 9, 11

Ubon Ratchathani Museum

The museum building here, previously a royal palace, contains exhibits from Isaan history, including its prehistory.

✉ Thanon Kheuan Thani, Ubon Ratchathani 🕐 Daily 9–12, 1–4 ✋ Inexpensive

Vimanmek Palace

The largest golden teakwood building in the world contains a superb collection of Ratanakosin-period objects (➤ 94).

✉ Thanon U-Thong Nai, Bangkok ☎ 022 816 880 🕐 Daily 9.30–4.30 ✋ Moderate 🚌 10

Exploring

Many of Thailand's highlights are not just the best of their kind in the country, but in the world. The islands' white-sand beaches and turquoise waters rival those of the Caribbean; the historical cities of Sukhothai and Ayutthaya are World Heritage Sites; and the diving is some of the best on the planet.

Most visitors land in the exciting and exhausting megalopolis of Bangkok before travelling onwards. Memorable journeys can be made into the mountains or buzzing past 'James Bond Island' in a traditional long-tail boat in Ao Phang-nga.

Riverside retreats are found throughout the country, from the peaceful towns on the northern border of the Mekong River to the floating lodges of Kanchanaburi. Even Bangkok's Chao Phraya River offers relief from the city.

Central Thailand

The broad, fertile plains of Central Thailand form the traditional heartland of old Siam, as they have since the Thai capital moved south from Sukhothai to Ayutthaya in the mid-14th century. Central Thailand, dominated by Bangkok, is the political powerhouse of the country. It provides the national language – Thai – which is spoken throughout the kingdom and understood everywhere, even by those whose first language is a regional dialect (such as the Northern Thai people) or a distinct minority language (as in the hill tribes).

Although perhaps the least scenically attractive region of Thailand, the central plains feature not only Bangkok but the ancient royal cities of Ayutthaya and Lopburi, where fascinating ruins reflect the country's past. Kanchanaburi, in the west, is a charming rural idyll just a couple of hours from the bustle of the capital; then there are the delightful floating markets, most notably at Damnoen Saduak.

Bangkok

When Siam's King Rama I established his new capital on a bend in the Chao Phraya River in 1782, he chose an easily defensible site where an old fort, called Bang Makok, or Bangkok for short, already existed. This name, although of venerable age, means 'place of olive plums', and was deemed insufficiently noble for a royal city. Accordingly, when the capital was first consecrated, it was given a new title which is still the longest place name in the world:

Krungthepmahanakhonbowonrattanakosinmahintaraay utthayamahadilokpopnopparatratchathaniburiromudo mratchaniwetmahasathanamonpimanavatansathirsakk athatityavisnukamprasit.

In English, this may be rendered: 'Great City of Angels, City of Immortals, Magnificent Jewelled City of the God Indra, Seat of the King of Ayutthaya, City of Gleaming Temples, City of the King's Most Excellent Palace and Dominions, Home of Vishnu and All the Gods'.

It is a tongue-twister, even for Thais, who shorten it to 'Krungthep' or the 'City of Angels' in everyday speech. The international community, following the preference of foreign ambassadors to the Chakri court, uses 'Bangkok'.

With a population of around 10 million, Bangkok is about 30 times larger than Nakhon Ratchasima or Chiang Mai, Thailand's next largest towns. It has a reputation for traffic jams, although the situation is improving yearly. It is a city of culture, haute cuisine and a throbbing nightlife, while still being safe and welcoming.

One of the stranger features of Bangkok is the absence of any single centre. The old royal city, built within three concentric canals on Ratanakosin Island, is the cultural and historical heart. Downtown Silom Road and the surrounding area are the equivalent of Bangkok's Wall Street – here are the major banking and trading institutions, as well as, near Silom's eastern end, the world-famous entertainment area Patpong Road, now known as much for its night market as for its neon lights and go-go bars. Sukhumvit Road, stretching away east towards Pattaya and the Gulf Coast, is a shopper's paradise, as well as a preferred location for many expatriate residents and mid-budget visitors.

Bangkok has become a city of gleaming shopping malls, best exemplified by the Mahboonkrong Centre, World Trade Centre and the region around Siam Square. Yet it is also still a city of canals, dominated by the great Chao Phraya River, which neatly bisects the Thai capital on its way to the nearby Gulf of Siam.

✚ 16H

BANG KHU WIANG FLOATING MARKET

Few experiences are more authentically Thai than a visit to a floating market. The best known is at Bang Khu Wiang in Thonburi, on the west bank of the Chao Phraya River. Water-borne commerce, most of which is conducted by women, starts at the crack of dawn and goes on for usually no more than two or three hours. To see Bang Khu Wiang, charter a long-tail boat from Tha Chang on Bangkok's Ratanakosin Island at about 6am.

There was a time, especially in the flat and well-watered central plains, when most commerce was water-borne. This is no longer true – canals have been filled in and built over, roads and covered markets have been constructed and scarcely a town in Thailand is without supermarkets and shopping malls. Floating markets – *talaat naam* in Thai – are now perceived to be a useful and lucrative tourist attraction.

✚ *Bangkok 3f* ✉ Bang Khu Wiang, Thonburi ☎ 013 747 616 🕔 Daily 4–7.30am 💷 Free 🚤 Long-tail boat from pier near Wat Phra Kaeo ❓ There is also another floating market near Bangkok at Damnoen Saduak (➤ 98).

BANGKOK'S CANALS AND RIVER

Bangkok was built on a bend in the Maenam Chao Phraya or 'River of Kings'. It had few roads, but was criss-crossed by canals, called *khlong* in Thai. In Thonburi, to the west of the river, a network of canals has survived. These were – and are – active canals, now used for commerce, commuting and tourist rides on long-tail speedboats. Easily chartered at any of the numerous piers, the long-tail boats dart up narrow canals, enabling passengers to explore little-known riverside communities. Alternatively, visitors can dine in state aboard a converted rice barge as it sails past majestic Wat Arun and the Grand Palace (➤ 40–41). The regular ferry service that runs throughout the city all day is the cheapest way to explore the Chao Phraya.

Sunset Cruise

✉ Marriott Royal Garden Riverside Hotel, Thanon Charoen Nakhon
☎ 024 760 021 🕙 Daily 5.30pm 🖐 Moderate

Riverside Company (dinner cruises)

✉ From Krungthon Bridge, Thanon Ratchawithi ☎ 024 340 090
🕙 Daily 7.30pm 🖐 Moderate

CHATUCHAK WEEKEND MARKET

See pages 36–37.

ERAWAN SHRINE

Many shrines are scattered throughout Bangkok but the most famous is dedicated to the four-headed Hindu deity Brahma (*Phra Prohm* in Thai). Constructed to dispel bad luck during the building of the Erawan Hotel in the 1950s, the shrine proved an immense success and believers still flock to pay their respects from all over the city. The atmosphere is rich with the fragrance of jasmine and incense, and elegant shrine dancers perform to a traditional Thai orchestra whenever someone pays them to do so. Entry is free but most visitors offer some flowers and incense; many believe that those who do so will be blessed with good luck and return to the 'City of Angels'. The shrine's statue of Brahma was destroyed by a hammer-wielding fanatic in 2006. He was beaten to death by enraged bystanders and the statue was rapidly replaced.

🕂 *Bangkok 7c* ✉ Thanon Ploenchit 🕙 Daily 🖐 Free 🍽 Cafés, Sogo Department Store 🚌 4, 5 🚇 E1 Chidlom Station

a walk around Chinatown

Explore the hidden temples of Chinatown, past apothecaries and colourful food stalls. Set off mid-afternoon, stopping for cocktails at dusk and ending with a taste of Little India.

Take the River Express boat to the Tha Ratchawong pier and walk up Ratchawong road for about 300m (327yds), past the motorcycle couriers and taxis. Turn right at the food stalls where a blue sign announces Soi Wanit 1.

This tiny alley, also known as Sampeng Lane, is the heart of Chinatown. Although barely wide enough for two people, load-bearing carts and motorbikes percariously weave their way through here. Once infamous for opium dens and gambling houses, fine Chinese silks and computer games are the wares of today.

Walk for two blocks past the 100-year-old Tang To Kang gold shop before turning left down Soi 16.

This alley is lined with sacks of rice crackers, tea and dried mushrooms, and stalls selling exotic local delicacies.

Cross the main road of Thanon Yaowarat and turn left along Thanon Charoen Krung (New Road). Halfway down this block on the right is the bustling temple of Wat Mangkon Kamalawat (Dragon Flower Temple).

The temple combines elements of Buddhism, Confucianism and Taoism, featuring both Chinese characters and Buddhist images.

Turn right as you come out of the temple and take the first left down the side street of Thanon Mangkon.

On the corner of Thanon Yaowarat, the Old Market is actually a modern complex of shopping stalls. Head upstairs for a professional reflexology treatment.

Turn right on to the main street of Thanon Yaowarat, and stop in at the Grand Chinese Princess Hotel.

The revolving restaurant and 'club lounge' on the 25th floor has a good view of the city lights. A few blocks further down on the right, antiques have now replaced the stolen goods for sale at Nakhon Kasen (Thieves' Market).

Cross over the bridge and turn left at the major road junction on to Thanon Chakraphet. This is Little India.

Follow the green sign to the Sikh temple (said to be the largest outside India) via a small tangle of market stalls. Then return to Thanon Chakraphet with its Indian restaurants and confectionery shops.

Distance 2.5km (1.5 miles) one way
Time 2–3 hours
Start/End point River Express Stop, Tha Ratchawong/Thanon Chakraphet 🚑 *Bangkok 3c* 🚌 7, 9, 11 ❓ River Express boats do not run in the evening, and many stalls close on the weekend

GRAND PALACE
See pages 40–41.

KHAO SAN ROAD
The street circus that is Khao San Road attracts tourists from around the world. Squeezed into a strip of under a kilometre are stalls three-deep selling clothes, food and souvenirs, as well as a maze of streets with cramped, basic travellers' accommodation. Although it is very much youth and budget orientated and crawling with backpackers, Khao San Road is always lively and friendly and offers comforting international relief when Bangkok gets too much.

This is where to come for an English breakfast, restaurants showing American films and English- and other-language books. The city's cheapest Internet connections are found here and travel agents fight for attention. Towards the beginning of the evening the music cranks up and the street becomes a riot of neon. Tourists eat banana pancakes in the street pursued by a constant parade of *tuk-tuks* and vendors.

✚ *Bangkok 3e*

JIM THOMPSON'S HOUSE

American businessman Jim Thompson set up in Thailand shortly after World War II and, almost single-handedly, revived the traditional Thai silk industry. This avid collector of antiquities, not just from Thailand but from Myanmar (Burma), Laos and Cambodia, built a magnificent house (actually several traditional central Thai wooden houses) at the end of a quiet lane by the banks of the Saen Saep Canal. Thompson disappeared mysteriously in Malaysia in 1967 but his elegant house has become a trust property.

➕ *Bangkok 6d* ✉ Soi Kasemsan 2, off Thanon Rama I ☎ 022 167 368 🕐 Mon–Sat 9–5 ✋ Moderate 🚇 National Stadium 🚌 8

NATIONAL MUSEUM

This is one of the largest and best-stocked museums in Southeast Asia, with a remarkable collection of objects from all periods of known 'Thai' history – that is, from the Ban Chiang civilization more than 4,000 years ago, through the Mon and Khmer periods, to the eventual immigration and settlement of the various Thai-speaking peoples from about AD900 onwards. As might be expected, the displays on the golden eras of Thai history – the Sukhothai and Ayutthaya periods – are particularly strong. The museum is well maintained and well presented, and regular guided tours are available.

➕ *Bangkok 2d* ✉ Thanon Na Phra That ☎ 022 241 370 🕐 Wed–Sun 9–4 ✋ Inexpensive 🍴 Wang Ngar Restaurant 🚌 7, 9, 11, 39

ORIENTAL HOTEL

Situated by the banks of the Chao Phraya River, the Oriental consistently rates in international surveys of the top five hotels in the world. Although an expensive place to stay, the Oriental offers excellent restaurants with riverside views and, most interestingly, a 'Writers' Room', once frequented by Joseph Conrad, Somerset Maugham, Noel Coward and Graham Greene.

➕ *Bangkok 4a* ✉ 48 Soi Oriental ☎ 026 599 000 🚊 S6 Saphan Taksin Station 🚌 76, 77

VIMANMEK PALACE

Originally constructed for King Chulalongkorn in 1868, Vimanmek was moved to its present location near Dusit Palace in 1910. A three-storey mansion comprising more than 80 rooms, Vimanmek is reputedly the largest golden teak building in the world – the cost of assembling a similar structure today would be astronomical. The interior contains an extensive collection of early Ratanakosin dynasty objects and antiques from the late 19th century.

➕ *Bangkok 4f* ✉ Thanon U-Thong Nai ☎ 026 286 300 🕐 Daily 9.30–3 ✋ Moderate 🚌 10

WANG SUAN PHAKKARD

The 'Lettuce Farm Palace', as this charming building is known as in Thai, was the residence of Princess Chumbot of Nakhon Sawan in the 1950s. An important scion of the ruling Thai royal family, Princess Chumbot was an eminent art collector and patron of Thai culture. Like Jim Thompson's House, the complex contains magnificent artistic treasures, including a fine lacquered pavilion dating from the late Ayutthaya period. Its beautifully landscaped gardens are a tranquil oasis in downtown Bangkok.

➕ *Bangkok 7d* ✉ 352 Thanon Sri Ayutthaya 🕐 Mon–Sat 9–4 ✋ Moderate 🚊 N2 Phya Thai Station 🚌 2, 3, 4

What to See in Central Thailand

AYUTTHAYA

In 1351 King Ramathibodi established his new capital at a former Khmer outpost on an island in the Chao Phraya River, symbolizing both the permanent transfer of Siamese power from Sukhothai to the south and the decline of the Cambodian Empire. He called his new city Ayutthaya – in Sanskrit 'unassailable' – after the town of Ayodhya in India. For the next 416 years Ayutthaya was the capital of Siam, finally proving all too assailable when it was captured by Burmese armies in 1767.

The new Siamese leader, King Taksin, moved his capital to Thonburi, from where it was transferred to Bangkok after Taksin's execution in 1782. Many of the new buildings in Bangkok employed materials floated downstream by raft from the ruins of Ayutthaya but the once-splendid city still retains an aura of royalty and some remarkable historical monuments. It is easy to visit from Bangkok – a popular way to do so is by luxurious riverboat, dining en route and stopping to visit King Chulalongkorn's palace at **Bang Pa In.**

An excellent way to gain an impression of the size and grandeur of Ayutthaya's majestic ruins is to rent a local long-tail boat and make a complete circuit of the island on which the city stands.

In the northeastern part of Ayutthaya, the **Chan Kasem Palace National Museum** displays Buddhist art and treasures. Built by King Maha Thammarat (1569–90) for his son, the palace was destroyed by the Burmese in 1767 but restored by King Mongkut in the mid-19th century.

Ayutthaya's largest museum, the **Chao Sam Phraya National Museum,** is in the middle of town. The collection includes many of the best pieces to have survived the Burmese sack of Ayutthaya, especially Thai Buddhist sculpture and religious

imagery. Books on religious art and Ayutthaya's history are for sale here.

Ayutthaya is full of old temples, but **Wat Mongkhon Bophit** is rather special because of its huge, awe-inspiring black Buddha image. Cast in the 15th century, this unique work of art was exposed to the elements for many years, but since 1956 has been protected by a brick and stucco building. Entering the building and looking up into the gilded eyes of the huge black Buddha figure can leave quite an impression.

🔵 16G ✉ 86km (53 miles) north of Bangkok 🚌 Regular air-conditioned buses from Bangkok 🚆 Ayutthaya
ℹ️ Thanon Rotchana ☎ 035 261 044

Bang Pa In
✉ 20km (12 miles) south of Ayutthaya 🕐 Daily 8.30–4.30 ✋ Moderate

Chan Kasem Palace National Museum
✉ Thanon U Thong, Ayutthaya 🕐 Wed–Sun 9–12, 1–4 ✋ Inexpensive
🍴 Chainam (£) 🚐 *Songthaew, tuk-tuk*

Chao Sam Phraya National Museum
✉ Thanon Rotchana, Ayutthaya 🕐 Wed–Sun 9–4 ✋ Inexpensive
🚐 *Songthaew, tuk-tuk*

Wat Mongkhon Bophit
✉ Thanon Si Sanphet, Ayutthaya 🕐 Daily 8–6.30 ✋ Free 🚐 *Songthaew, tuk-tuk*

AYUTTHAYA HISTORICAL PARK

This UNESCO World Heritage Site covers most of the island that makes up the old city and has many temples worth visiting. At least half a day is required – a full day, with lunch by the river would be ideal. Bicycles can be rented near the entrance.

🔵 16G ✉ 86km (53 miles) north of Bangkok ☎ 035 245 123–4 🕐 Daily 9–4
✋ Free 🚐 *Songthaew, tuk-tuk* from Thanon Si Sanphet ❓ Among the many temples worth visting are Wat Mongkhon Bophit, Wat Phra Si Sanphet, Wat Phra Mahathat, Wat Ratburana and Wat Yai Chai Mongkhon

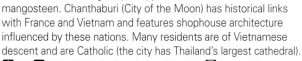

CHANTHABURI

This busy riverside commercial hub specializing in the gem trade (both local and imported from the Pailin region in Cambodia) is home to 40,000 people. It is famous for its fine fruits, especially durian, rambutan, langsat, pineapple and mangosteen. Chanthaburi (City of the Moon) has historical links with France and Vietnam and features shophouse architecture influenced by these nations. Many residents are of Vietnamese descent and are Catholic (the city has Thailand's largest cathedral).

✚ 17J ✉ 330km (205 miles) southeast of Bangkok 🚌 Regular air-conditioned buses from Bangkok

DAMNOEN SADUAK FLOATING MARKET

Take a water taxi to the floating market on Khlong Damnoen Saduak in Ratchaburi Province, 104km (64 miles) southwest of Bangkok (after first going to Damnoen Saduak by bus or taxi).

Markets such as this are the traditional way to shop, dating back to when the canals were the major thoroughfares. One boat may be piled high with fresh coconuts, another packed with garlic; others sell a mix of fruit and vegetables. All the while, floating restaurants dole out noodle soup to market workers and tourists.

As with all morning markets in Thailand, it is best to arrive as

early as possible (certainly by 8.30am). Even at dawn, the market is busy, as boats laden with an extensive range of fruit, vegetables and flowers jostle for space on the crowded waterway.

✚ 15H ✉ Damnoen Saduak, 104km (64 miles) southwest of Bangkok 🕐 Daily from sunrise 🍴 Snacks sold from boats

🚌 78 from southern bus terminal, Bangkok 🚤 Water taxi from Damnoen Saduak to Talaat Phitak

THE EASTERN GULF COAST

Thailand's eastern gulf coast is something of a contradiction. On the one hand, it is the nation's most developed commercial region, with Laem Chabang deep-water port, oil refineries and an ugly industrial zone stretching east and south from Bangkok for almost 100km (62 miles). On the other hand, it has some of the finest beaches in Thailand, the delightful island of Ko Samet and, in and around Ko Chang (Elephant Island), one of the least-developed, most pristine archipelagos in Southeast Asia.

One of the area's attractions is its proximity to Bangkok, but this has a downside. Good roads make it readily accessible – there is an elevated four-lane motorway stretching as far as Chonburi. Resorts nearer to Bangkok are generally packed, particularly on weekends. There is not a lot to interest visitors in Chachoengsao and Chonburi, and most people prefer to head south to the coastal resorts. The first of these, Si Racha, is largely a Thai destination, while the next, Pattaya, is geared towards foreign visitors. Next comes Rayong, jumping-off point for Ko Samet and increasingly a resort town in its own right.

Further east is the fascinating old town of Chanthaburi. The road east, Sukhumvit Highway, ends in a tapering finger of Thailand that culminates in the quintessentially Thai city of Trat (certainly not a resort town), the Ko Chang archipelago and the small town of Hat Lek, an official crossing point into Cambodia.

✚ 16K ✉ East of Bangkok 🚌 Regular air-conditioned buses from Bangkok to all towns

ERAWAN NATIONAL PARK

This park covers 550sq km (215sq miles) of unspoiled wilderness in the Kwai Yai river valley. It is a great place for walking and swimming, with well-marked trails and numerous waterfalls, the highest of which is named after the mythical Hindu-Buddhist three-headed elephant Erawan.

The best time to visit is during the rainy season when the falls are at their most impressive, but, being quite close to Bangkok, the park is a popular draw for local visitors and is best avoided during *songkran* (➤ 24), the traditional Thai New Year each April, if you are seeking solitude and empty spaces.

✚ 14G ✉ 65km (40 miles) northwest of Kanchanaburi ☎ 025 797 223 ✋ Expensive

JEATH WAR MUSEUM

The acronym by which this interesting war museum is known represents the first letters of the combatant nations – Japan, England, Australia, America, Thailand and Holland. A friendly Thai monk called Phra Tongproh, who speaks some

English, runs the museum and he can be very helpful in showing visitors around. The museum is based on one of the *atap* huts in which Allied prisoners of war were held during World War II. Exhibits on display include paintings by former prisoners, photographs and various weapons, such as Japanese swords.

✚ 15H ✉ Thanon Wissutharangsi, Kanchanaburi 🕐 Daily 8.30–6
✋ Inexpensive

KAMPHAENG PHET HISTORICAL PARK

In the 13th century this ancient riverside city was part of the Kingdom of Sukhothai. Even before this, it was an important centre in the Khmer Empire. Today it is a provincial town whose partly restored old buildings form a historical park and a World Heritage Site. The star attraction is Wat Phra Kaeo, with its weather-sculpted Buddha statues. The Emerald Buddha, Thailand's most important Buddha image, was once held here, but is now kept in Wat Phra Kaeo in Bangkok (➤ 40–41).

The monastery of Wat Phrathat and San Phra Isuan Shrine are also worth a look. The **National Museum** has archaeological finds from all over Thailand as well as from excavations in Kamphaeng Phet. Next door is the **Provincial Museum,** displaying collections introducing the history and traditions of Kamphaeng Phet province. A group of forest *(arunyik)* temples to the north of the walled city were built by meditating monks.

✚ 7D 🕐 Daily 8–4.30 ✋ Free
ℹ Thanon Phahalyotin ☎ 055 514 341
National Museum
🕐 Wed–Sun 8–4 ✋ Inexpensive
Provincial Museum
🕐 Wed–Sun 8–4 ✋ Inexpensive

KANCHANABURI

The small town of Kanchanaburi is a delightful place, ironically with a worldwide reputation for the notorious 'bridge over the river Kwai' – **Death Railway Bridge.** During World War II, the invading Japanese forces decided to build a supply railway link across the difficult country between the Thai and Burmese rail systems. Hundreds of thousands of people were forced to work under appalling conditions, resulting in the deaths of an estimated 16,000 Allied prisoners of war and 100,000 indentured Asians.

The original bridge was destroyed by Allied bombing during 1945 and only rebuilt after the war. Today little remains of the original railway to Myanmar (Burma), although trains can still run within Thailand as far as Nam Tok via the infamous 'Hellfire Pass'.

Most visitors to Kanchanaburi go to see the restored bridge and perhaps to pay their respects at the war cemeteries – the **Kanchanaburi Allied War Cemetery** in the north-central part of town, and the more distant **Chung Kai Allied War Cemetery** on the west bank of the Kwai River. Reaching this cemetery involves a short boat trip and a pleasant stroll through unspoiled rural land. The well-cared-for cemeteries contain the graves of thousands of Dutch, British, French, New Zealand and Australian soldiers.

'Kan' has good accommodation and a wide choice of restaurants. Like most Thai cities, it has a city pillar (the Lak Muang) at its

symbolic heart. Found near the post office, the pillar has a bulbous-shaped tip, often likened to a lotus but generally accepted as phallic in origin, which devotees have covered in gold leaf.

One of the more unusual sights in Kanchanaburi, indeed in Thailand, is at Wat Tham Mongkon Thong, the 'Temple of the Cave of the Golden Dragon'. The temple itself is nothing special but is famed for its **'floating nun'** – a Thai *mae chii*, or nun, floating on her back while meditating in a pool of water. Pious Buddhists come to witness this act and to receive the nun's blessings.

Kanchanaburi is a rewarding destination at any time of the year, but the best time is in late November and early December when a series of sound and light shows based around the restored bridge is held daily.

✚ 15H ✉ 130km (81 miles) west of Bangkok 🍽 Mae Nam (BB) 🚌 Regular air-conditioned buses from Bangkok 🚉 Kanchanaburi Station

Death Railway Bridge
✉ Thanon Mae Nam Kwai, Kanchanaburi
🕐 Unrestricted 👋 Free 🚌 *Songthaew*
❓ River Kwai Bridge Week, late Nov

Allied War Cemeteries
✉ Thanon Saengchuto, Kanchanaburi
🕐 Unrestricted 👋 Free 🚌 Minibus No.2

The floating nun
✉ Thanon Chukkadon, across Mae Klong River, Kanchanaburi 🕐 Daily 7–6 👋 Free (donation)

KO CHANG

Ko Chang (Elephant Island) is the biggest of more than 40 islands in the Gulf of Siam, off the coast of Trat, Thailand's most southeasterly province. It is Thailand's second largest island after Phuket but almost completely undeveloped by comparison. Until recently it had no paved roads, and accommodation is still limited to simple bungalows scattered along the coast. Best reached by ferry from Laem Ngop, it is a wonderland of unspoiled tropical rainforest, pristine beaches and clear seas – but light on the water sports available at more developed resorts.

➕ 18K ✉ 350km (217 miles) southeast of Bangkok
🍴 Excellent beach cafés 🚌 Air-conditioned buses from Bangkok to Laem Ngop

KO SAMET

This narrow finger of an island lying just a short distance off the coast of Rayong is still, despite its increasing popularity, a relaxing destination. Distinguished by white, crisp beaches, it offers sunbathing, swimming, snorkelling and excellent seafood. For nightlife, go to Pattaya instead.

➕ 17J ✉ 220km (136 miles) southeast of Bangkok, Gulf of Thailand
✋ Cheap 🍴 Excellent beach cafés 🚌 Regular buses from Bangkok to Ban Phe, where ferries operate regular services to the island

NAKHON PATHOM

Phra Pathom *Chedi* (pagoda) is the main attraction in Nakhon Pathom (56km/35 miles west of Bangkok), and is said to be the tallest Buddhist monument in the world. It dominates the skyline all around. A whistle-stop visit to the *chedi* is usually squeezed in to a tour from Bangkok on the way back from the Damnoen Saduak Floating Markets and Kanchanaburi Town.

Although there is not much else here to see for visitors, Nakhon Pathom is thought to be Thailand's oldest town, and the place where Buddhism first entered the country. There are two museums in the town, both confusingly called Phra Pathom Museum. The newer one has 6th- to 11th-century local artefacts and the other, a small room, is crowded with amulets, Chinese ceramics, Thai musical instruments and gems.

✚ 15H ✉ 56km (35 miles) west of Bangkok

PATTAYA

Visitors usually develop very definite opinions about this place. Long billed as Thailand's top resort, the beaches are poor compared with Phuket, Ko Samui and Ko Samet. On the other hand, the sheer number of hotels, restaurants and entertainment venues is staggering. Long infamous for its nightlife, the southern part of town is packed with bars and bar girls – there is a lively gay scene here, too. Northern Pattaya is more of a family destination, as is Jomtien Beach, stretching to the south of the city.

✚ 16J ✉ 147km (91 miles) southeast of Bangkok 🍴 Good restaurants
🚌 Bangkok Airport minibuses, regular air-conditioned buses
🚉 Pattaya Station ❓ Pattaya Festival, 12–19 Apr

a walk around Lopburi

The busy town of Lopburi, about 150km (93 miles) north of Bangkok, has a long history. Originally settled by Mon people, it was an important bastion of Dvaravati culture from as early as AD600, before being conquered, in turn, by the Khmer Empire and the Thais. In the mid-17th century Lopburi was used as a second capital by King Narai, who built a summer palace there.

These days, the town is overrun by monkeys – a tourist attraction in their own right.

Lopburi is divided into western and eastern sections. The former includes the old town as well as earlier Khmer ruins. To the east the new town is the site of the provincial offices and the best hotels.

Start a walk around Lopburi at Narai's palace, which was abandoned soon after his death and not restored until the mid-19th century. The palace exhibits both French and Khmer architectural influences, as well as Central Thai.

Enter Narai's palace through the main gate (Pratu Phayakkha) and stroll through the well-kept grounds. To the left are the elephant stables.

The palace took 12 years to build (1665–77), and comprised a royal temple, harem buildings, audience halls, administrative buildings and kitchens. The Lopburi National Museum here

has an outstanding collection of Mon and Khmer period statuary. To the east of the palace grounds is Wat Phra Si Ratana Mahathat, a 12th-century Khmer temple restored by the Fine Arts Department.

Walk east a short distance to the railroad station, then north along Thanon Na Phra Kan.

To the right is Wat Nakhon Kosa, a 12th-century Khmer temple, which may once have been dedicated to Hinduism.

Keep walking north across the roundabout.

In the middle of the roundabout is San Phra Kan, a shrine dedicated to Kala, the Hindu god of death and time. The shrine swarms with the monkeys for which Lopburi is famous. They can be bad-tempered so be careful.

Continue north along Thanon Na Phra Kan.

On the right is Prang Sam Yot, another Khmer-built Hindu temple that has long since been dedicated to Buddhism.

✚ 8F
Distance 2.5km (1.5 miles) **Time** 1–2 hours
Start point Narai's Palace 🚐 *Songthaew*
End point Prang Sam Yot
Lunch Boon Bakery (B) ✉ Thanon Na Phra Kan

SANGKHLA BURI

Around 20km (12 miles) from the Thai-Burmese border, Sangkhla Buri is perhaps the nicest place to spend the night in this area. Populated with mostly Mon and Karen people, it is more Burmese than Thai and very little English is spoken. Its focus is a reservoir that was created by the damming of the Khwae Noi River. You can still see parts of the drowned villages and trees. A daily morning market at Wat Wangwiwekaram sells crafts from Burma, China and India. There are canoeing trips on the Kheuan Khao Laem Reservoir and Thailand's longest wooden bridge leads over the body of water to a welcoming Mon settlement.

✛ 6F

THREE PAGODAS PASS

This outpost on the border takes its name from the trio of pagodas supposedly built in the 18th century as a demonstration of peace between Thailand and Burma (modern Myanmar). Thailand traditionally prevented foreigners crossing into Burma from the pass due to border fighting with rebels. Things are generally peaceful now and if the border is open you can visit the Burmese village of Payathonzu for the day, although it's a good idea to check the current situation first.

The market in Payathonzu has exotic goods from neighbouring countries. On both sides of the border you can find hand-embroidered textiles from India, precious gems from Cambodia and intricate Indonesian woodcarvings. Hard bargaining is expected.

✛ 6F

HOTELS

BANGKOK

Asia (BBB)

Conveniently situated for Siam Square and the World Trade Centre. Close to the banks of Saen Saep Canal, making travel to Sukhumvit by boat an easy option.

✉ 296 Thanon Phayathai ☎ 022 150 808; www.asiahotel.co.th
🚌 79 🚊 N1 Ratchathewi Station

Banyan Tree (BBB)

A landmark highrise in the central Bangkok, this luxurious hotel soars more than 60 storeys above the city and claims to have Asia's highest bar, aptly named Vertigo.

✉ 21/100 Thanon South Sathorn ☎ 026 791 200; www.banyantree.com
🚌 530

Dusit Thani (BBB)

Situated in the heart of Bangkok's Silom Road business district, this incredibly sumptuous hotel has eight restaurants and six bars. There are stunning views from the rooftop Tiara Restaurant.

✉ Thanon Rama IV ☎ 022 360 450–9; www.dusit.com 🚌 112, 502, 504
🚊 S2 Saladaeng Station

Four Seasons (BBB)

A centrally located luxury hotel offering every conceivable amenity from ballroom dancing to yoga.

✉ 155 Thanon Ratchadamri ☎ 022 516 127;
www.fourseasons.com/bangkok 🚌 504, 505, 514 🚊 S1 Ratchadamri Station

Grand Hyatt Erawan (BBB)

Luxurious, centrally located and perfect for the World Trade Centre and Ploenchit. Nearby is the venerable Erawan Shrine (➤ 89).

✉ 494 Thanon Ratchadamri ☎ 022 541 234; www.bangkok.hyatt.com
🚌 504, 505, 514 🚊 E1 Chidlom Station

Mandarin Bangkok (BBB)

Fresh, airy rooms and all the facilities associated with a luxury hotel. Reasonable room rates for the quality.

✉ 662 Thanon Rama IV ☎ 022 380 230; www.mandarin-bkk.com 🚌 4, 21, 25, 29, 34, 40, 73, 109

Oriental (BBB)

Long Bangkok's top hotel, the Oriental has aquired many rivals in terms of luxury, but not character (➤ 94).

✉ 48 Soi Oriental ☎ 026 599 000; www.mandarinoriental.com 🚌 76, 77 🚆 S6 Saphan Taksin Station

Rembrandt (BBB)

Luxury facilities including six restaurants; Mexican and Indian cuisine are featured. Five minutes by car from Queen Sirikit Convention Centre – on a good day.

✉ Soi 18 Thanon Sukhumvit ☎ 022 617 100; www.rembrandtbkk.com 🚌 501, 508, 515 🚆 E4 Asoke Station

Royal (B)

One of Bangkok's oldest and most venerable hotels, close to the Grand Palace. In 1992, this was the scene of some of the worst excesses against pro-democracy demonstrators by the army.

✉ 2 Thanon Ratchadamnoen Klang ☎ 022 229 111 🚌 7, 507, 508

Shangri-La (BBB)

One of Bangkok's best hotels; even offers helicopter transfer service to the airport. Serves high tea.

✉ 89 Soi Wat Suan Phlu ☎ 022 367 777; www.shangri-la.com 🚌 76, 77 🚆 S6 Saphan Thaksin Station

Sunrise Residence (BB)

In a quiet lane of the Silom district, this friendly boutique hotel is a short walk from Patpong nightlife and some of the city's best restaurants. Includes free Internet access.

✉ 1101 Saladaeng 1/1, Thanon Saladaeng, Silom ☎ 026 362 500; www.thesunriseresidence.com 🚆 S2 Saladaeng, metro Silom

White Lodge (B)
A small, friendly place and good value. Close to Siam Square, Mahboonkrong Shopping Centre and Jim Thompson's house.
✉ 36/8 Soi Kasem San 1 ☎ 022 153 041 🚌 73, 79, 204 🚇 Siam Station

AYUTTHAYA
Ayutthaya Grand (BB)
Comfortable hotel slightly away from the main part of town. Nightclub, coffee shop and pool.
✉ 55/5 Thanon Rotchana ☎ 035 335 484–5; www.aygy.co.th

Ayutthaya Riverside (BBB)
Probably the best hotel in Ayutthaya, with views of the river and town. Chinese restaurant, bowling alley and snooker club.
✉ 27/2 Thanon Rotchana ☎ 035 243 139; www.ayu/riverside.com

U-Thong Inn (BB)
Well positioned for all the main historical sights. Facilities include a pool and a sauna room. New wing is better value than the old.
✉ 210 Thanon Rotchana ☎ 035 242 236–9; www.uthonginn.com

KANCHANABURI
Felix Kanchanaburi Swissotel River Kwai (BBB)
Luxurious resort beside the River Kwai. Beautifully landscaped gardens plus tennis courts and large swimming pools.
✉ 9/1 Moo 3 Thamakhan ☎ 034 551 000; www.felixriverkwai.co.th

Kasem Island Resort (B)
Thatched cottages and houseboats to the south of the town on a small island. Offers rafting, fishing and a pleasant bar.
✉ Kasem Island, near Thanon Chukkadon ☎ 034 513 359 or 022 553 604

River Kwai Hotel (BB)
An old favourite away from the river in the town. Well-appointed rooms, disco, coffee shop and pool.
✉ 284/3–16 Thanon Saengchuto ☎ 034 513 348; www.riverkwai.co.th

KO SAMET
Samet Ville Resort (BB)
Private and chic, well away from the sprawl of bungalows on other more developed beaches. Fan-cooled and air-conditioned bungalows.

✉ Wai Bay ☎ 038 651 681

Vongdeuan Resort (BB)
One of the better resorts on the island. Air-conditioned bungalows with running water in beautiful (but noisy) Wong Deuan Bay.

✉ Wong Deuan Bay ☎ 038 651 777; www.vongdeuan.com

LOPBURI
Lopburi Inn Resort (B)
Situated out of town to the west, Lopburi's newest and best hotel. Excellent facilities including sauna, fitness centre and large pool.

✉ 144 Tambon Tha Sala ☎ 036 420 777; www.lopburiinnresort.com

PATTAYA
Pattaya Centre Hotel (BB)
All rooms at this modern highrise hotel on Pattaya's beachfront have views of the sea. Facilities include a large swimming pool, a snooker room and in-house massage.

✉ 240 M.10, Soi 12, Beach Road ☎ 038 425 877–8; www.freeservers.com

Royal Cliff Beach Hotel (BBB)
Overlooking South Pattaya and Jomtien Bay, this is one of Pattaya's oldest and best hotels. Sports facilities and eight excellent restaurants.

✉ 378 Thanon Pratamnak ☎ 038 250 421–3; www.royalcliff.com

RESTAURANTS

BANGKOK
Bei Otto (BB)
A German restaurant with a *bierhaus*, delicatessen and bakery.

✉ 1 Sukhumvit Soi 20 ☎ 022 620 892 🕐 Lunch, dinner 🚌 501, 508, 511 🚇 E4 Asoke Station

Bourbon Street (BB)

Cajun-Creole cookery (red beans and rice, gumbo, jambalaya). Mexican buffet on Tuesday nights.

✉ Washington Square, Sukhumvit Soi 22 ☎ 022 590 328 🕐 Breakfast, lunch, dinner 🚌 501, 508, 511 🚇 E5 Phrom Phong Station

Bussaracum (BBB)

See page 58.

Coyote (BBB)

Thai restaurants on busy Convent Road have made room for a newcomer from Mexico, a fashionable combination of smart bar (serving 75 different margaritas) and a restaurant offering such 'fusion' dishes as taquitoes filled with Thai soft-shelled crab.

✉ Sivadon Building, 1/2 Convent Road ☎ 026 312 325 🚇 S2 Saladaeng

Gianni's (BB)

Simple, excellent Italian dishes such as angel-hair pasta with lobster. Two- and three-course set lunches.

✉ 34/1 Soi Tonson, Thanon Ploenchit ☎ 022 521 619 🕐 Lunch, dinner; closed Sun 🚌 502, 504 🚇 E2 Ploenchit Station

Huntsman (BB)

British-style pub serving popular dishes such as steak and kidney pie. Beef buffet on Monday evenings.

✉ The Landmark Hotel, 138 Thanon Sukhumvit ☎ 022 540 404 🕐 Lunch, dinner 🚌 501, 508, 511 🚇 E3 Nana Station

Indus (BB)

Bangkok's top Indian restaurant, serving light dishes from the north in a cool, brick-walled dining room. The home-made sorbets are a dream.

✉ 71 Thanon Sukhumvit, Soi 26 ☎ 022 584 900 🚌 501, 508, 511 🚇 E5 Phrom Phong

Lemongrass (BB)

See page 58.

Mahboonkrong Food Centre (B)

A large range of food stalls providing Thai and international food in a bustling atmosphere.

✉ Mahboonkrong Shopping Centre, corner of Thanon Phayathai and Thanon Rama I 🕐 Daily 10–9 🚌 73, 79, 204 🚈 Siam Station

Mojos Bar & Grill (BB)

Great jazz accompanies your dining on weekend evenings at this very individual restaurant in Bangkok's lively Soi 33. 'Happy hour' extends to 8pm, and every evening has its special theme (on Thursdays your dining companion eats for free).

✉ 10/19–20 Thanon Sukhumvit, Soi 33 ☎ 022 608 430 🚌 501, 508, 511 🚈 E5 Phrom Phong

Scala Shark's Fin (BBB)

The best shark's fin soup in Bangkok, and other Chinese specials.

✉ 483–485 Thanon Yaowarat ☎ 026 230 183 🕐 Lunch, dinner 🚌 4, 5 🚈 Mahboonkrong

Spice Market (BBB)

One of the best Thai restaurants in Bangkok, in a replica Thai spice shop.

✉ Four Seasons Hotel, 155 Thanon Ratchadamri ☎ 022 516 127 🕐 Lunch, dinner 🚌 504, 505, 514 🚈 S1 Ratchadamri Station

AYUTTHAYA

Chainam (B)

Good Thai and Chinese food at reasonable prices in a simple riverside setting, at the rear of a general store.

✉ Thanon U Thong, near Chan Kasem Palace ☎ 035 252 013 🕐 Breakfast, lunch, dinner

Phae Krung Kao (BB)

Floating on the Pa Sak River, this restaurant specializes in seafood, chicken and pork dishes. Chinese delicacies are also available.

✉ Moo 2 Thanon U Thong ☎ 035 241 555 🕐 Lunch, dinner

CHANTHABURI
Chomlom (BB)
Freshly caught fish is prominent on the menu of this open-air riverside restaurant. The seabass fish cakes are particularly tasty.
✉ Tambol Tarat ☎ 038 323 684 🕐 Lunch, dinner

KANCHANABURI
Mae Nam (BB)
This pleasant, large, floating restaurant specializes in fish and seafood. Meat and vegetarian dishes are also available.
✉ On the river at the end of Thanon Lak Muang ☎ 034 512 811
🕐 Breakfast, lunch, dinner

Punnee Café and Bar (B)
Popular with expatriate residents, serving Western-style Thai food and Thai-style European dishes plus 'the coldest beer in town'.
✉ Thanon Ban Neua ☎ 034 513 503 🕐 Breakfast, lunch, dinner

LOPBURI
Bualang (BB)
This is a favorite with some members of the Thai royal family, whose ancestors created the 'royal Thai cuisine' which still forms the basis of the restaurant menu. The soft-shelled crab with pepper and garlic is a Bualang speciality.
✉ 46/1 Thanon Pahalyotin, Tambol Thasala ☎ 036 323 684

PATTAYA
Lobster Pot (BBB)
See page 59.

Pan Pan San Dominico (BBB)
Italian food of the highest order, serving possibly the best veal in Thailand. From the menu to the décor everything at Pan Pan is first-rate.
✉ Thanon Theprasit ☎ 038 251 874 🕐 Lunch, dinner

PIC Kitchen (BB)

Fine Thai cuisine served in traditional style at low wooden tables in elegant teak houses. There is a separate air-conditioned section. Recommended.

⊠ Soi 5, Pattaya Beach Road ☎ 038 428 387 ⊕ Lunch, dinner

Ruen Thai (BB)

A series of wooden pavilions is the setting for classical Thai dancing and high-quality Thai food. The restaurant has children's facilities including a playground.

⊠ 485/3 Pattaya 2nd Road ☎ 038 425 911 ⊕ Lunch, dinner

SHOPPING

CDS AND BOOKS

Thailand's three bookshop chains, Asia Books, Bookazine and Duang Kamol (DK) Book House, are good for new books and magazines. Asia Books, with Bangkok's best selection of English-language titles on Asia, is at Bangkok and Thailand's international airports; DK Books and Bookazine are in most towns and cities.

Asia Books

New English-language novels and large format coffee-table books on Asia.

Main Branch ⊠ Soi 15, 221 Thanon Sukhumvit, Bangkok ☎ 022 527 277 🚌 136, 185 🚇 E4 Asoke Station

Landmark Plaza ⊠ Floors 1 and 3, Sois 2 and 3 Thanon Sukhumvit, Bangkok ☎ 022 525 839 🚌 501, 508, 515 🚇 E3 Nana Station

World Trade Centre ⊠ Junction of Thanon Ratch-adamri and Thanon Rama I, Bangkok 🚌 204, 205 🚇 E1 Chidlom Station

Bookazine (Siam)

Excellent selection of international magazines.

⊠ 286 Siam Square, Thanon Rama I, Bangkok 🚌 73, 79, 205 🚇 Siam Station

Chatuchak Weekend Market

Second-hand English magazines and novels (➤ 36–37).

DK Book House

English-language novels and computer books (main branch).
Latest fiction titles (Sukhumvit branch).

Main Branch ✉ 244–6 Soi 2, Siam Square, Bangkok ☎ 022 511 467
🚌 73, 79, 205 🚇 Siam Station

Sukhumvit branch ✉ Thanon Sukhumvit, Bangkok 🚌 501, 508, 511
🚇 E3 Nana Station

Elite Book House

Second-hand books and periodicals.

✉ 593/5 Thanon Sukhumvit, Bangkok ☎ 022 580 221 🚌 501, 508, 511
🚇 Phromphong

Shaman Books

Second-hand novels, maps and guidebooks; new books.

✉ 71 Thanon Khao San, Bangkok ☎ 026 290 418 🚌 503

DEPARTMENT STORES

Central Chidlom

The Chidlom branch of the Central department store chain is
conveniently located next to the Chidlom Skytrain station. It has
the complete range of reasonably priced Central goods, from
clothing to household accessories and souvenirs.

✉ Thanon Plon Chit, Bangkok 🚌 4, 5 🚇 E1 Chidlom Station

Mahboonkrong Center

One of Bangkok's oldest shopping centres, bordering central Siam
Square, and still a favourite with Thais, who flock here to browse
the innumerable boutiques and stalls, watch a movie and eat at
one of the many traditional restaurants.

✉ Junction of Thanon Rama 1 and Thanon Phayathai, Bangkok 🚌 16, 25, 73,
79, 204, 501, 508 🚇 Siam Station W1

Mike Shopping Mall

Mainly a clothes arcade, but there is a small supermarket within
the complex.

✉ 262 Moo 10, Pattaya Beach Road, Pattaya

Siam Discovery Center

Aptly named because of the sheer variety of quality goods
for shoppers to discover, from designer clothes to the latest
electronics. The upper floors have an excellent variety of
restaurants and a multi-screen cinema complex.

✉ Siam Square, Bangkok 🚌 16, 25, 73, 79, 204, 501, 508 🚉 National
Stadium Station W1

World Trade Centre

See page 69.

GEMS, JEWELLERY AND SILK
Asian Institute of Gemmological Sciences

Learn the art of gemmology. The institute will also authenticate
any gems you may have.

✉ 33rd Floor, Jewellery Trade Centre, 919/1 Thanon Silom, Bangkok
☎ 022 674 315–9 🚌 2, 4, 5

Gemopolis

See page 68.

Jim Thompson Silk Shop

See page 68.

Johnny's Gems

A long-established place for set jewellery.

✉ 199 Thanon Fuang Nakhon, off Thanon Charoen Krung, Bangkok
☎ 022 244 065 🚌 4

Rasi Sayam

Handicrafts from all over the country, notably silk from Isaan and
northern Thailand, are sold in this historic old house off busy
Thanon Sukhumvit. Closed Sun.

✉ 32 Thanon Sukhumvit, Soi 23, Bangkok ☎ 022 584 195 🚉 Sukhumvit
🚌 501, 508, 511 🚉 Asok

Shinawatra Thai Silk

A fine selection of silk products and other textiles. They have another branch in Chiang Mai.

✉ Thanon Sathorn Tai, near Soi Suan Plu, Bangkok ☎ 022 580 295–7
🕐 Mon–Sat 🚌 17, 22, 62

MARKETS, ANTIQUES AND HANDICRAFTS

Chatuchak Weekend Market

This sprawling market sells everything from Buddha images and ceramics to musical instruments, plus a vast range of clothing. On an average weekend, about 200,000 people visit daily (➤ 36–37).

✉ Southern end of Chatuchak Park, off Thanon Phahonyothin, Bangkok
🕐 Sat–Sun 8–6 🚇 Chatuchak 🚊 N8 Mor Chit Station

Gaysorn Plaza

See page 68.

Pratunam Market

A large market complex hidden away from the main roads surrounding it. Specializes in newly designed clothing at exceptionally cheap prices.

✉ Junction of Thanon Phetburi and Thanon Ratchaprarop, Bangkok
🚌 4, 5, 11, 12, 13

ENTERTAINMENT

NIGHTCLUBS AND BARS

Alcazar

The ultimate drag-queen show, complete with extravagant sets.

✉ 78/14 Thanon Pattaya 2, Pattaya ☎ 038 428 746 🕐 Daily evening shows 6.30, 8 and 9.30 (and 11pm on Sat)

Bar Baska

Retro building given a Balinese feel. Very popular on weekends.

✉ 82–83 Ekamai Soi 22, Bangkok ☎ 027 114 748–9 🕐 Daily 6pm–2am
🚌 1, 8 🚊 Ekamai

Mambo Cabaret

No visit to Bangkok is complete without a night out at a transvestite show, and this is one of the best and most respectable. There are two shows nightly, at 8.30pm and 11pm.

✉ Washington Square, 496 Thanon Sukhumvit, Bangkok ☎ 022 595 715
🚌 501, 508, 511 🚇 E5 Phrom Pong

Radio City

Sandwiched between some of the raunchiest bars of Bangkok's renowned Patpong district, this laid-back music bar is perfectly respectable and boasts one of the city's best showbands.

✉ Patpong Soi 1, Bangkok ☎ No telephone 🚌 2, 4, 5 🚇 S2 Saladaeng Station

Renoir

Hostesses at this refined and friendly bar in Sukhumvit's lively Soi 33 wear a differently coloured but invariably elegant evening dress each night of the week. Happy hours extend until 9pm, and on some evenings there's a free buffet.

✉ Thanon Sukhumvit, Soi 33, Bangkok ☎ No telephone 🚌 501, 508, 511
🚇 E5 Phrom Pong

Pattaya Palladium

A large entertainment complex with reputedly the largest disco in Thailand.

✉ 78/33–35 Thanon Pattaya 2, Pattaya ☎ 038 424 922 🕐 Daily 11am–12 midnight

Phuture

Large hi-tech disco popular with affluent young Thais and expatriates. Live music events occasionally.

✉ Chao Phraya Park Hotel, 91/9 Thanon Ratchadapisek, Bangkok ☎ 026 938 022 🕐 Daily 9pm–2am 🚌 4, 10, 29

Saxophone Pub

An established venue for live jazz; also has some blues and rock.

✉ 3/8 Victory Monument, Thanon Phayathai, Bangkok ☎ 022 465 472
🕐 Daily 6pm–2am 🚌 2, 3, 9, 10, 13 🚇 N3 Victory Monument Station

THEATRE
National Theatre
Traditional performances of both *khōn* and *lákhon*. *Khōn* is a formal masked dance drama based around the Ramakien – Thailand's national epic; *lákhon* is a more general form of dance.

✉ Thanon Na Phra Tat, near Phra Pin Klao Bridge, Bangkok ☎ 022 241 342
🕐 7 performances monthly 🚌 7, 9, 11, 39

SPORT

Bike & Travel
Based in Pathum Thani, Bike & Travel offers cycling and canoe tours, including trips to Khao Yai National Park.

✉ 802/756 River Park, Moo 12, Thanon Phahon Yothin, Pathum Thani, Bangkok ☎ 029 900 274

Kan Tarat Golf Course
Set between the runways of Bangkok International Airport and the military airport, this tight, 18-hole Air Force-run course sounds dangerous but is actually great fun.

✉ Don Muang Airport, Bangkok ☎ 025 343 840

Lumpini Boxing Stadium
Here you can watch the world's top *Muay Thai* (Thai boxing) exponents. Bouts can be quite bloody. Fights take place on Tuesdays and Fridays from 6.30pm, Saturday afternoons 5–8pm, and Saturday nights from 8.30pm.

✉ Thanon Rama IV, near Lumpini Park, Bangkok ☎ 022 514 303 🕐 Tue, Fri 6.30–11, Sat 5.30–8pm and 8.30pm–midnight 🚌 7

Royal Bangkok Sports Club
Horse-racing on alternate Sundays; always a full card of races.

✉ 1 Thanon Henri Dunant, Bangkok ☎ 026 281 810 🕐 Sun 12.30–6 🚌 4, 5
🚇 S1 Ratchadamri Station

Royal Turf Club
A full card of races on the other Sunday to the Royal Bangkok
Sports Club (➤ 121). Big events include the Derby Cup and the
President's Cup.

✉ 183 Thanon Phitsanulok, Bangkok ☎ 022 800 020 🕔 Sun 12.30–6
🚌 5, 9, 11

SP Bowling
A new, state-of-the-art, 28-lane ten-pin bowling alley with karaoke
rooms on site.

✉ Floor 7, Mahboonkrong Center (MBK), 444 Thanon Phayathai, Bangkok
☎ 026 117 171 🕔 Sun–Thu 10am–1am, Fri–Sat 10am–2am 🚇 Ma Boon
Krong 🚌 1, 2, 8

Southern Thailand

Southern, peninsular Thailand is a narrow strip of land, likened to an elephant's trunk, which joins the bulk of mainland Southeast Asia to the Malay Peninsula via the Isthmus of Kra. It is a beautiful region of coconut palms and rubber plantations, azure lagoons and sharp karst outcrops. Some Thais believe southerners are more fiery in disposition than their fellow citizens. There is little to indicate this to the visitor except perhaps the spicier food and the speed at which the local dialect of Thai is spoken.

In this part of Thailand, Buddhist culture persists as far south as Nakhon Si Thammarat, then Islam begins to appear. By the time you reach Phuket, the blend of traditions is obvious. Chinese settlers, too, have left a major mark on this region. Finally, in the four 'deep south' provinces of Pattani, Yala, Narathiwat and Satun, Islam becomes predominant and Malay is the main local language. Here Thai and Malay worlds meet and merge in an unusual synthesis of cultures.

Phuket

The island of Phuket lies in the Andaman Sea just off the coast of Phang-nga Province and is joined to the mainland by a short causeway. At 810sq km (316sq miles), it is Thailand's largest island and has developed in the last 25 years into one of the most luxurious and elaborate beach resorts in the whole of Southeast Asia. The name Phuket derives from the Malay word *bukit* (hill) and is pronounced 'Pooket'.

In past centuries, Phuket was an important centre for import and export on the eastern shore of the Bay of Bengal, handling shipping and dealing with sailors from the Arab and Malay worlds, India, Burma, China and, of course, Siam. By the 16th century, it was also well known to Europeans, as first Portuguese and Dutch, then English and French, sailed there.

Phuket enjoyed an unprecedented surge in wealth when tin was found in large quantities just offshore. Miners and businessmen arrived from the provinces of south China, adding a considerable Sinitic element to the island's already mixed population.

It was not until about 1975 that Phuket's potential for tourism was finally realized. Although more expensive than almost any other resort in Thailand, it is still reasonable by international standards, especially in view of its beauty and amenities.

✚ 13Q ✉ Phuket Island, 862km (534 miles) south of Bangkok 🍴 Excellent restaurants 🚌 *Songthaews* and *tuk-tuks* run to all beaches from Phuket Town ✈ Phuket International Airport ❓ Vegetarian Festival, Phuket Town, Oct

BEACHES

Phuket is all about beaches – it has some of the best in the world. Nearly all the major ones are on the western shore of the island, running from Mai Khao in the north to Nai Harn in the south. The best known is Patong, which has a lively night-time scene not unlike that of Pattaya. Then there are more sedate beaches like Kata and Karon. All share Phuket's wonderful coastline on the Andaman Sea, offer excellent accommodation and food and make the perfect place for a beach-based holiday. There are fewer beaches on the island's east coast, but near the southern tip of the island at Cape Phrom Thep – famous for its legendary sunsets – Rawai Beach deserves a mention. Phuket and neighbouring islands such as Phi Phi were badly hit by the 2004 tsunami, but very little evidence of the appalling devastation suffered by the region is to be seen today. Recovery was swift and complete.

PHI PHI MARINE NATIONAL PARK

Usually referred to as Phi Phi Island, this marine park actually consists of two islands, Phi Phi Don and the smaller, virtually uninhabited Phi Phi Leh. Located equidistantly from Phuket and Krabi, the islands can be reached by boat in about two hours. It is possible to stay in bungalow accommodation or, increasingly, in trendy hotels on Phi Phi Don. There is no accommodation on Phi Phi Leh. Famous for their clear waters, coral reefs and white, sandy beaches (the setting for the 2000 Leonardo DiCaprio film *The Beach*), the islands remain remarkably lovely despite ill-controlled development. For a spectacular view of Phi Phi Don, climb the well-signposted path from the double-sided beachfront area known as The Village. The path passes a tiny Thai settlement and leads to the deserted beaches of Ao Lanti and Ao Koh Bakao.

🚩 14R ✉ Andaman Sea, 40km (25 miles) south of Krabi 🍴 Good cafés in Ton Sai Village ⛴ Ferries from Krabi and Phuket

SEA GYPSY VILLAGE

Phuket, with the islands of the Mergui Archipelago stretching north into Myanmar (Burma), is home to an unusual indigenous people: the *chao thalae* or 'people of the sea', often called 'sea gypsies'. Now reduced to a tiny minority of the Phuket population, they traditionally make their living from the sea, spending most of their lives in boats. Their village is on Ko Sire Island, connected to Phuket by a causeway.

🚼 3E 📧 Sea Gypsy Village east of Phuket Town on Ko Sire Island 🍴 Gypsy World Seafood Restaurant 🚌 *Songthaew* or *tuk-tuk*

What to See in Southern Thailand

ANG THONG MARINE NATIONAL PARK

Comprising 40 small islands, Ang Thong is a spectacular combination of karst outcrops, azure lagoons, perfect beaches and swaying coconut palms. The tiny archipelago is uninhabited and best visited as a day trip from Ko Samui. Climb to the top of the most accessible peak (240m/787ft) and marvel at the spectacular natural beauty around you.

✚ 15N ✉ 31km (19 miles) northwest of Ko Samui 🚢 Ferries from Ko Samui

CHA-AM

This small, friendly town is a popular weekend destination for people living in Bangkok. It has a long beach lined with casuarina trees, excellent seafood (as throughout the peninsular south) and a wide choice of accommodation. Cha-Am can get pretty busy on weekends, particularly during school holidays, but the beach is generally quiet on weekdays.

✚ 15J ✉ 180km (112 miles) south of Bangkok 🚌 Buses from Bangkok
🚉 Cha-Am Station
ℹ Phetkasem Highway ☎ 032 471 005

HUA HIN

Hua Hin, just 25km (16 miles) south of Cha-Am, is the antithesis of Pattaya, its brash sister resort on the opposite side of the Bight of Bangkok. This trendy, family-orientated destination is Thailand's oldest beach resort. King Rama VII built a palace called Glai Gangwon or 'Far from Cares' there in 1928. Hua Hin is also well known for its renowned Hua Hin Railway Hotel, a fine colonial-style building renamed Hotel Sofitel Central.

✚ 15J ✉ 205km (127 miles) south of Bangkok 🍴 Railway Restaurant (BBB)
🚌 Buses from Bangkok 🚉 Direct from Hualamphong Station, Bangkok
ℹ Municipal Office, Phetkasem Road ☎ 032 511 047

KHAO SOK NATIONAL PARK

See pages 42–43.

KO PHA-NGAN

The second largest island in the Samui archipelago, Ko Pha-Ngan lies a half-hour ferry ride north of Samui, and is much less developed – though this is changing fast. Like Samui, the island has fine beaches, a densely wooded and mountainous interior and several beautiful waterfalls. But being cheaper, Pha-Ngan draws more budget visitors and fewer high-rollers. It has no 'capital' to speak of – the main town and port at Thong Sala is tiny. Most visitors head to the beaches and stay in bungalows, although hotels and more upmarket accommodation are available.

✚ 15N ✉ 15km (9 miles) north of Ko Samui, Gulf of Thailand 🚌 Regular air-conditioned buses from Bangkok to Surat Thani 🚉 Surat Thani 🚢 Night ferry from Ban Don, boats from Ko Samui ✈ Regular flights from Bangkok to Ko Samui Airport

KO SAMUI

The Samui archipelago became a budget-visitor's paradise back in the 1970s, but has since become considerably more stylish. The main island of the group, Ko Samui, is Thailand's premier beach resort along with Phuket. There is not much to do at Nathon, the main town and port for arrival by ferry. The chief seaside destinations are Chaweng Beach on the island's east coast and Lamai on the south coast. The island is ringed by a well-maintained road, and the hilly interior is packed with coconut trees. There are more than 10 flights a day to Ko Samui from Bangkok, an indication of this lovely island's appeal and popularity.

✚ 15N ✉ Gulf of Thailand 🍴 Good seafood restaurants 🚌 Buses from Bangkok to Surat Thani 🚉 Surat Thani 🚢 Ferries from Surat Thani and Ban Don ✈ Regular flights from Bangkok ℹ Nathon ☎ 077 288 818

KO TAO

Ko Tao (Turtle Island) is the most northerly and least developed
destination in the Samui archipelago. As on its sister islands, the
main industries are fishing, coconut farming and, increasingly,
tourism. Since it takes several hours to reach the island from the
mainland, most visitors stay for several days. It is an ideal place to
lie back and relax, with good swimming, diving and snorkelling, as
well as the cheapest accommodation in the group.

➕ 15N ✉ 40km (25 miles) northwest of Ko Pha-Ngan 🚆 Chumphon
and Surat Thani 🚢 Ferries from Chumphon, Surat Thani, Ko Pha-Ngan and
Ko Samui

KRABI

This fast-developing provincial capital is known for eco-tourism.
Local agencies arrange half-day trips to mangrove swamps, visits
to the nearby Khao Nor Chuchi rainforest and sea-kayaking trips
along the Andaman coast. The best beaches are out of the town,
which is located on a riverine estuary. For excellent swimming and
sunbathing, try Hat Ton Sai, Hat Rai Leh and Hat Tham Phra Nang,
all fine beaches easily reached by boat. Krabi also has regular ferry
services to Phi Phi Island (➤ 126).

➕ 14Q ✉ 815km (505 miles) south of Bangkok 🍴 May and Mark (BB)
🚌 Regular air-conditioned buses from Bangkok 🚢 Boat trips to Ko Phi Phi
and Ko Lanta Yai ℹ Utarakit Thanon ☎ 076 211 036

NAKHON SI THAMMARAT

In many ways Nakhon Si Thammarat, although smaller than Hat Yai, is the real capital of the south. Relatively few tourists visit this historic city, despite the fact that the remains of the old city walls and some of the temples – notably the magnificent Wat Phra Mahathat – are well worth seeing. There are quite a few mosques, too, a sure sign of the south, although most Muslims here speak Thai not Malay. Just to the north of town is a lovely, casuarina-lined beach called Hat Sa Bua. It can be crowded on weekends but makes a great mid-week retreat, and has some excellent seafood restaurants.

✚ 15Q ✉ 780km (484 miles) south of Bangkok 🍴 Krua Nakhon (BB) 🚌 Buses from Bangkok 🚆 Nakhon Si Thammarat ✈ 5km (3 miles) north of town ❓ Chak Phra Pak Tai festival, Wat Phra Mahathat, mid-Oct

ℹ Off Thanon Ratchadamnoen ☎ 075 346 515

NARATHIWAT

The capital of the southernmost province in Thailand, Narathiwat is famous for its mangoes and songbirds. The people are almost exclusively Malay-speaking Muslims (though Thai nationals) and this is reflected in the food and general culture. Most officials are Thai and the commercial district is dominated by ethnic Chinese; otherwise it is almost as if you had crossed the border into Malaysia. The usual Gulf formula applies – quiet, clean beaches, excellent seafood and friendly people – but, because of its distance from Bangkok, there are few tourists.

✚ 17S ✉ 1,150km (713 miles) south of Bangkok 🍴 Food stalls serving southern curries (B) 🚌 Regular air-conditioned buses from Bangkok ✈ Narathiwat Airport, links from Bangkok and Phuket ❓ Narathiwat Fair, mid-Sep

PATTANI

Like Narathiwat, Pattani is over-
whelmingly populated by Malay-speaking
Muslims, although it has an influential
ethnic Chinese community. Pattani is an
important fishing port, once capital of an
independent (if small) kingdom, and
memories of its independence still linger
in local minds. There is plenty of
accommodation but only one beach –
Laem Tachi, 10km (6 miles) long, to the north.

✚ 17S ✉ 1,055km (654 miles) south of Bangkok 🚌 Regular air-conditioned
buses from Bangkok ✈ Hat Yai Airport, 110km (68 miles) away with bus
service provided ❓ Chao Mae Lim Ko Niao Fair, late Feb or early Mar

AO PHANG-NGA

See pages 46–47.

PRACHUAP KHIRI KHAN

About 80km (50 miles) down the Gulf coast from the popular resort of Hua Hin, the small town of Prachuap Khiri Khan is far enough from Bangkok to discourage day-trippers and even weekenders. There are fine beaches to the north and the south of town; the latter, at Ao Prachuap, is 8km (5 miles) long and very pretty. An interesting side trip is a visit to Ao Bang Nang Lom, just north of Ao Prachuap, where wooden fishing boats are still made in the traditional way. Visitors may also climb Khao Chong Krajok or 'mirror mountain' for a fine view of the town and bay.

🚉 15K ✉ 285km (177 miles) south of Bangkok 🍴 Pan Phochana (BB) 🚌 Regular air-conditioned buses from Bangkok 🚆 Direct links from Hualamphong Station, Bangkok ✉ 8km (5 miles) north of Hua Hin

RANONG

The town of Ranong, near the banks of the Pakchan River, is not very interesting in itself but makes an ideal base for a day trip to the nearby Myanmar town of Kawthoung, also known as Victoria Point. Regular boats leave the pier on the Thai side of the river.

➕ 14N ✉ 645km (400 miles) south of Bangkok ✋ Day pass to enter Myanmar (Burma): inexpensive 🍴 Ranong Garden Hotel (BB) 🚌 Air-conditioned buses from Bangkok ✈ Ranong Airport, 20km (12 miles) south

SIMILAN ISLANDS

See pages 50–51.

SONGKHLA

An attractive beach resort, Songkhla is a quietly cultured place. Apart from its fascinating national museum in a century-old Sino-Portuguese-style building, it boasts Songkhla Nakarin, the most prestigious university in southern Thailand, several colleges and, on nearby Ko Yo (Yo Island), the Institute of Southern Thai Studies. Southern Thai cuisine is almost always excellent but Songkhla is famed particularly for its seafood. For those interested in wildlife, Khukhut Waterbird Sanctuary is 30km (19 miles) north of town.

➕ 16R ✉ 950km (589 miles) south of Bangkok 🍴 Seafood restaurants 🚌 Air-conditioned buses from Bangkok 🚆 Hat Yai Station, 26km (16-mile) taxi ride to Songkhla ✈ Hat Yai Airport, taxi to Songkhla

HOTELS

HUA HIN

Sofitel Central (BBB)

A fine old colonial-style hotel by the beach, with a topiary garden. This is the place filmed as the French Embassy in Phnom Penh in the film *The Killing Fields*.

✉ 1 Thanon Damnoen Kasem ☎ 032 512 021–35

KO SAMUI

Central Samui Beach Resort (BBB)

In a beautiful garden setting, towards the middle of Chaweng Beach, offering a health centre and tennis courts. Just 15 minutes' drive from the airport.

✉ 38/2 Moo 3 Borpud, Chaweng Beach ☎ 077 230 500; www.centralhotelsresorts.com

Coral Cove Chalet (BB)

Beautifully located resort set in a cove framed by coconut palms. Good swimming pool and excellent restaurant.

✉ 210 Coral Cove Beach, Lamai ☎ 077 422 260–1; www.coralcovechalet.com

Imperial Boat House (BBB)

A unique resort with beautifully decorated old teak rice barges for accommodation and a boat-shaped pool. Extensive facilities.

✉ 83 Moo 5 Tambon Bophut ☎ 077 425 041–52; www.imperialhotels.com

KRABI

Krabi Resort (BB)

Stay in a luxury bungalow and watch the sun set over the outlying islands in the Andaman Sea, then party at the resort's videotheque.

✉ Moo 2 Tambon Ao Nang ☎ 075 637 031

PHUKET
Amanpuri Resort (BBB)
Perhaps Phuket's most exclusive resort. Isolated and tranquil, it
attracts the cream of Thai society. Yachts are available for cruising.
✉ Pansea Beach ☎ 076 324 333; www.amanresorts.com

Diamond Cliff Resort (BBB)
At the northern end of Patong Beach, set in extensive grounds
overlooking Patong Bay. Two good restaurants.
✉ 284 Thanon Prabarimi, Patong ☎ 076 340 501–6; www.diamondcliff.com

Dusit Laguna Resort (BBB)
Between a beautiful lagoon and the sea. A large resort with
superb restaurants and health facilities.
✉ 390 Thanon Sri Sunthorn, Cherngtalay ☎ 076 324 320–32;
www.dusit.com

Felix Karon Phuket (BB)
At the northern end of Karon Beach. Good children's facilities.
Great Southern Thai restaurant.
✉ 4/8 Thanon Patak, Karon Beach ☎ 076 396 666–75;
www.felixphuket.com

Marina Cottage (BB)
Surrounded by coconut palms at the southern end of Karon Beach.
✉ 119 Mu 4 Thanon Patak, Karon Beach ☎ 076 330 625;
www.marinaphuket.com

SONGKHLA
Samila Beach (BBB)
Located on Samila Beach, next to the Songkhla golf course.
✉ 8 Thanon Ratchadamnoen ☎ 074 440 222; www.bphotelsgroup.com

RESTAURANTS

HAT YAI

Hua Lee (BB)

Popular with the local Chinese for its superb shark's fin and bird's-nest soups. Open until very late.

✉ Thanon Niphat Uthit 3 ☎ No telephone 🕔 Lunch, dinner

HUA HIN

Railway Restaurant (BBB)

Decorated in the style of Hua Hin Railway Station in the 1920s. Thai, French, Italian and Chinese buffets.

✉ Hotel Sofitel, 1 Thanon Damnoen Kasem ☎ 032 512 021 🕔 Breakfast, lunch, dinner

Rim Nam (BB)

Live classical Thai music accompanies excellent Thai food served in a traditional antique Thai-style setting. The kaeng khiaw wan (green curry) is excellent.

✉ 43/1 Petchkasem Beach Road ☎ 032 520 250 🕔 Breakfast, lunch, dinner

Saeng Thai (BB)

The oldest restaurant in Hua Hin. Reliable seafood coupled with good service. Open-air on the seafront.

✉ Thanon Naresdamri (near the pier) ☎ 032 512 144 🕔 Breakfast, lunch, dinner

KO SAMUI

Captain's Choice (BBB)

See page 58.

Happy Elephant (B)

Thai dishes like grilled prawns and sweet tamarind sauce with prawn cakes grilled on fresh sugar cane sticks. Excellent seafood.

✉ 19/1 Moo 1 Bophut ☎ 077 245 347 🕔 Lunch, dinner

Kantara (BB)

Seaside restaurant offering Thai and continental cuisine. Classical Thai dancing in the evenings. Large, reasonably priced lunchtime buffet.

✉ Blue Lagoon Hotel, 99 Moo 2, Chaweng Beach ☎ 077 422 037

🕐 Breakfast, lunch, dinner

Pakarang (BB)

Dine indoors surrounded by paintings of Ko Samui, or outside under a bougainvillea trellis. The chef makes no attempt to reduce the Thai flavours unless requested.

✉ 9 Moo 2 Tambon Bophut ☎ 077 422 223; www.coralbay.net

🕐 Breakfast, lunch, dinner

KRABI
Sala Thai (BB)

Freshly caught seafood is barbecued nightly at this beachfront restaurant at Krabi's Ao Nang. Crabmeat soup is a highly recommended starter.

✉ 132 Moo 2, Thanon Hat, Ao Nang ☎ 075 637 024 🕐 Lunch, dinner

NAKHON SI THAMMARAT
Khrua Nakhon (B)

Enjoy authentic southern Thai dishes in an open-style restaurant. Special dishes include kao yum (Southern Thai salad) and kanom jeen (Chinese noodles).

✉ Bovorn Bazaar, Thanon Ratchadamnoen ☎ 075 317 197 🕐 Breakfast, lunch

PHUKET
Bluefin Tavern (BB)

Slightly away from Kata Beach, this pub serves dishes like Texas chilli and fish chowder, Cuban black bean soup, pastrami and roast beef sandwiches.

✉ 111/17 Thanon Taina, Kata Beach ☎ 076 330 856 🕐 Lunch, dinner

Kan Eng Seafood (BB)

Superb fresh Thai seafood; the curried seafood mousse is a must.
Diners make their own selection from the seafood on display.
Views over Chalong Bay yacht harbour.

✉ Chalong Bay ☎ 076 381 323 ◷ Lunch, dinner

Kiko (BBB)

Fine Japanese restaurant next to the beach with ingredients
freshly imported from Japan. Special dishes include sushi and
sashimi.

✉ Diamond Cliff Resort, 284 Thanon Prabarimi, Kalim Beach ☎ 076 340 501;
www.diamondcliff.com ◷ Lunch, dinner

Metropole Café (BB)

Comfortable à la carte dining in a smart setting. Choose from
imported beef steak, South Chinese cuisine or fresh seafood
prepared in southern Thai style.

✉ Metropole Hotel, 1 Soi Surin, Montri Road, Phuket Town ☎ 076 215 050
◷ Dinner

Pae Thip (BB)

One of the Pearl Village Resort's three classy restaurants, set in
the middle of a lake. Beautifully prepared Thai food, plus Japanese
and Korean dishes. Try the Korean barbecue, cooked at the table.

✉ Pearl Village Resort, Nai Yang Beach ☎ 076 327 006;
www.indigo-pearl.com ◷ Breakfast, lunch, dinner; closed Wed

Regatta Bar and Grill (BBB)

Superb *nouvelle cuisine* from the resident European chef. One of
Phuket's best restaurants, overlooking Nai Harn Bay. Live music.

✉ Phuket Yacht Club, Nai Harn Beach ☎ 076 381 156 ◷ Lunch, dinner

Sea Hag (BB)

An oasis of fine dining in Phuket's down-market Patong Beach
area. Thai and international dishes are on the extensive menu, and
the wines are good and moderately priced.

✉ Soi Permpong 3, Patong ☎ 076 341 111 ◷ Lunch, dinner

Tropica (BB)
See page 59.

RANONG
Palm Court (BB)
The best restaurant in town, part of the Jansom Thara Ranong Hotel. Dim sum and Chinese noodle dishes plus Thai food like kaeng matsaman (Muslim curry).
✉ 2/10 Thanon Phetkasem ☎ 077 811 510 🕒 Lunch, dinner

SHOPPING

ART
The Loft Art Gallery
A variety of contemporary art can be found in the upstairs section of this tastefully renovated shophouse. The downstairs houses a selection of Asian antiques.
✉ 36 Thanon Thalang, Phuket ☎ 076 258 160; www.theloft-antiques.com

BOOKS AND MAGAZINES
The Books
English-language magazines.
✉ 53–55 Phuket Road, Phuket

GEMS AND JEWELLERY
Pearl Centre
Phuket is a good source of fine quality pearls. The centre has some good bargains.
✉ 83 Ranong Road, Soi Phutorn, Phuket 🕒 Mon–Sat ☎ 076 211 707

SHOPPING CENTRE
Robinson Ocean Plaza
Clothes boutiques, fast-food restaurants and a large supermarket attached to a branch of Robinson's department store.
✉ Ong Sim Phai Road, Phuket Town

ENTERTAINMENT

BARS AND NIGHTCLUBS

Banana Discotheque

Dance club with an attached pub, popular with couples.

✉ 124 Thawiwong Road, Patong Beach, Phuket ☎ 076 340 301 🕓 Daily 9pm–2am

Reggae Pub

A large open-air dance floor swings to the latest sounds as well as reggae.

✉ Chaweng Beach, Ko Samui 🕓 Daily 10pm–2am

SPORT

Andaman Hooker Sport Fishing Charter

Phuket is a great place to go big-game fishing, with an abundance of marlin, sailfish and tuna in the waters. Andaman Hooker offers day trips or charter trips of up to five days.

✉ 6/6 Soi Suki Moo 9, Chalong Bay, Phuket ☎ 076 282 036

Ao Chalong Yacht Club

The club holds monthly yacht races and visitors to Phuket are welcome to join in.

✉ Chalong Bay, Phuket ☎ 076 381 914

Ao Nang Muay Thai

View Thailand's national sport, *Muay Thai* (Thai-style boxing), at the beach.

✉ Ao Nang Stadium, Ao Nang Beach, Krabi 🕓 Sat 8pm–1am

Big Game Fishing

Either go angling in the daytime off the coast of Ko Pha-Ngan or take a night boat and fish with the aid of spotlights. You can keep or sell what you haul in.

✉ AK Travel, 20/5 Moo 1, Choeng Mon Beach, Ko Samui ☎ 077 425 390

The Dive Shop

Two British diving instructors established this Ko Samui dive centre in 1992 and built it up into one of Southeast Asia's leading water sports businesses.

✉ Chaweng Beach Road, Ko Samui ☎ 077 230 232; www.thediveshop.net

Phuket Country Club

A magnificent 27-hole golf course with a driving range. Visitors are welcome.

✉ 80/1 Vichitsongkram Road, Kathu, Phuket ☎ 076 321 039

Scuba Cat Diving

Trips to the Similan and Surin islands, where it is occasionally possible to glimpse the world's largest fish, the whale shark, as well as other sea creatures.

✉ Patong Beach Road, Patong or Kata Beach (Kata main road), Phuket
☎ 076 345 246

Sea Canoe Thailand

Offers tours around scenic Phang-nga Bay in inflatable canoes, giving access to the bay's caves – something that is impossible with ordinary boats.

✉ 367/4 Yaowarat Road, Phuket ☎ 076 212 252

Northern Thailand

Northern Thailand has a different atmosphere to the rest of the kingdom. This is because the region did not come under the full control of Bangkok until the first decade of the 20th century. For several hundred years it existed as an independent state called Lan Na, or the 'Kingdom of a Million Rice Fields'. The traditions and language of the north developed independently from those of central Thailand. Its people even used to dress differently; the women wearing their hair long in contrast to the cropped locks of their Siamese counterparts, the men covering their bodies with intricate tattoos to ward off sickness and injury.

Diversions for visitors, too, are very different, from whitewater rafting to trekking on foot or elephant, while the cities, especially Chiang Mai, have perhaps the nation's loveliest temples. This land of forested mountains and lush valleys is populated by sophisticated Buddhist lowlanders and a wide range of hill tribes.

Chiang Mai

Founded more than seven centuries ago by King Mangrai the Great, Chiang Mai has remained the political and cultural heart of the north from the time of the independent Lan Na kingdom to the present. Lan Na passed through a golden age in the 14th and 15th centuries but in 1558 was conquered by the Burmese and became a vassal state. It was not until 1775 that Lord Kavila, the ruler of Lampang, the second largest city of the north, drove out the Burmese. By this time Chiang Mai was all but depopulated and tigers roamed at will within the deserted fortifications.

Kavila gave orders for the city to be abandoned completely between 1776 and 1796. In the latter year he resettled the city,

pronounced it his new capital, and began to restore the fortifications. The bastions, moats and remains of the city walls that contribute so much to the city's beauty date from this time. Over the next century Chiang Mai and the north became increasingly tied to Bangkok, and in 1932 the last vestiges of northern independence disappeared when the region became a province of Thailand.

As the north becomes more prosperous and the government in Bangkok

increasingly confident and secure, northerners have begun to reassert their culture. The heart of this movement and the acknowledged capital of the region is Chiang Mai, dubbed 'the Rose of the North'. The city has much to offer the visitor, from temples and historic monuments to fine restaurants and golden sunsets accentuated by Doi Suthep, its guardian mountain.
✚ 6B

BOR SANG UMBRELLA VILLAGE
This village is devoted to the manufacture and sale of painted and lacquered paper umbrellas. Almost every household seems to be involved in the business. Visitors can visit the many workshops to see how the umbrellas are made and take photos. Fans, silverware, bamboo and teak furniture, celadon and lacquerware are also made.
✚ 6B ✉ Route 1006, 9km (6 miles) east of Chiang Mai ⏰ Daily 7–5.30
🍴 On main street 🚌 *Songthaew* or *tuk-tuk* ✋ Free ❓ Festival, Jan

DOI INTHANON
See pages 38–39.

DOI SUTHEP

The mountain dominating Chiang Mai to the west has two peaks,
Doi Suthep and Doi Pui, which together constitute a national park.
The road to the summit leads past several waterfalls, most notably
– about 7km (4 miles) from town – the Monthatharn Falls, a picnic
spot. At the 14km (9-mile) road marker, about two-thirds of the
way up, is the beautiful and much revered Wat Phrathat Doi
Suthep. This temple, easily seen from Chiang Mai, provides great

views across the valley. Nearer the summit, the gardens of Phuping Palace can be a riot of colour from November to February.

✚ 6B ✉ 16km (10 miles) west of Chiang Mai 🕐 Temple daily 6–6; Palace Gardens Sat–Sun 8.30–12.30, 1–4 (closed when royal family in residence) 🍴 Cafés near the temple (B) 🚌 *Songthaews* from front of Chiang Mai University, Thanon Huay Kaew, and Wat Phra Singh in the Chiang Mai city centre

LAMPANG

The only city in Thailand that continues to use pony carts for transport (now mainly for sightseeing), Lampang is an hour's drive south of Chiang Mai. The north's second largest city prospered as a teak town in the 19th century when merchants moved there from Myanmar (Burma). Burmese influence is visible in the city's temples, at least four of which have Burmese abbots. The oldest part of town, with the most historic monuments, lies to the north of the River Wang, which runs through the city.

✚ 7C ✉ 92km (57 miles) south of Chiang Mai 🍴 Riverside Bar and Restaurant (BB) 🚌 Buses from Bangkok 🚉 Lampang Station ✈ Lampang Airport ❓ Elephant Kantoke Fair, Feb

LAMPHUN: WAT PHRA THAT HARIPUNCHAI

Just 30 minutes' drive south of Chiang Mai, Lamphun was founded in AD950 and is the oldest continually inhabited city in Thailand. The old Chiang Mai–Lamphun road is lined for several kilometres with 30m-high (98 ft) ancient yang trees. Dating from 1467, the stepped pyramid-shaped Suwanna *chedi* (pagoda) of the beautiful Wat Phra That Haripunchai is one of the few examples of Dvaravati Mon architecture surviving in Thailand. Nearby hangs a giant gong, reputed to be the largest in the world. Opposite the temple is the excellent Lamphun National Museum.

✚ 6B ✉ 26km (16 miles) south of Chiang Mai 🚌 Regular buses from Chiang Mai ❓ Longan Fair, Aug

NIGHT BAZAAR

Located in the heart of downtown Chiang Mai, this bustling, three-storey market sells every variety of hill-tribe craft, antique, pseudo-antique and souvenir, all at very reasonable prices and difficult to beat elsewhere. It is necessary to bargain, however. In addition to the night bazaar building there is a busy street market all along central Thanon Chang Khlan.

✚ 6B ✉ Thanon Chang Khlan, Chiang Mai 🕐 Daily 5–11 🍴 Bars and cafés down each edge of the bazaar 🚐 *Songthaews* 💲 Free

WAT PHRA THAT LAMPANG LUANG

See pages 54–55.

What to See in Northern Thailand

CHIANG RAI

An excellent way to travel to Chiang Rai, 'Gateway to the Golden Triangle', is to overnight at one of the comfortable riverside lodges in Thaton, 180km (112 miles) north of Chiang Mai. Follow the river – fast by long-tail boat, or slow by raft – to Chiang Rai. It has little of historic interest but a lot in the way of tourist facilities and is the main base for exploring the Golden Triangle region, where the borders of Myanmar (Burma), Laos and Thailand come together.

✚ 7A ✉ 180km (112 miles) north of Chiang Mai 🚍 Buses from Bangkok and Chiang Mai ✈ Chiang Rai Airport ❓ Lychee Fair, May ℹ Thanon Singhakhlai 448/16 ☎ 053 717 433

CHIANG SAEN AND THE GOLDEN TRIANGLE

The historic town of Chiang Saen, dating from the 12th century, is on the west bank of the Mekong River about 90 minutes' drive from Chiang Rai. Here you can explore the town's ruins, take a boat trip or sit and enjoy a cool drink while gazing across the river into nearby Laos. Just 10km (6 miles) north of Chiang Saen, by road along the bank of the river, is the one-street town of Sop Ruak, the heart of the infamous 'Golden Triangle' (Sam Liam Thong Kham), from where the Burmese drug lord Khun Sa once controlled the opium trade. Don't miss the fascinating Hall of Opium (▶ 81) just outside Sop Ruak on the road to Mae Sai.

✚ 7A ✉ 60km (37 miles) north of Chiang Rai 🍴 Border View (BB)
🚌 Regular air-conditioned buses from Chiang Mai and Chiang Rai
ℹ️ Thanon Phahonyothin 🕐 Mon–Sat 8.30–4.30 ☎ 053 744 674

MAE HONG SON

Once one of Thailand's remotest provinces, Mae Hong Son is now readily accessible by air from Chiang Mai, as well as by a wonderful loop drive through Mae Sariang and back via Pai (or vice versa). Although Thai citizens, most of the townsfolk are of Shan, Karen, Yunnanese Chinese or hill-tribe descent. The temples are Burmese in style and the pace of life slow.

✚ 5B ✉ 270km (167 miles) northwest of Chiang Mai going through Pai
🍴 Bai Fern (BB) 🚌 Regular air-conditioned buses from Chiang Mai
✖️ Mae Hong Son Airport ❓ Poi Sang Long, Mar

MAE SAI

The chief attraction of this small commercial enclave on the banks of the Sai River, about 90 minutes' drive from Chiang Rai, is Myanmar (Burma). It is possible to make a day trip across the river without a visa – a small charge applies at the border bridge – and stroll around the Myanmar border town of Thakhilek. The people are friendly and speak better English than the Thais but are palpably less well-off. By arrangement with a local tour office, visitors can also make a three-day round trip to Kengtung, the main city of the eastern Shan state of Myanmar.

➕ 7A ✉ 65km (40 miles) north of Chiang Rai 🍴 Pu Tawan Resort (B)

🚌 Regular air-conditioned buses from Chiang Rai, VIP bus to Bangkok

ℹ Thanon Singhakhlai 448/16, Chiang Rai ☎ 053 717 433

NAN

Until about 20 years ago Nan was considered 'unsafe' because of a smouldering communist insurgency in the province. It is still off the beaten track but quite safe to visit. This sleepy provincial capital, which only becomes busy in October and November when the annual dragon boat races are held, is remarkable for Wat Phumin, a temple rich in 19th-century murals painted by unknown artists that record scenes of secular and religious society in Nan 150 years ago.

✚ 8B ✉ 318km (197 miles) east of Chiang Mai 🍴 Siam Pochana (B)
🚌 Regular air-conditioned buses from Bangkok and Chiang Mai
✈ Nan Airport ❓ Lanna Boat Races, Oct–Nov

PHITSANULOK

Phitsanulok is an excellent base for exploring the nearby historical sites at Sukhothai, Si Satchanalai, Sawankhalok and even Kamphaeng Phet. It has some of the best accommodation and restaurants in the lower north, the latter especially along the banks of the Nam River which snakes through the town. Wat Phra Si Ratana Mahathat is the most important temple in Phitsanulok. Its main hall contains the Phra Phuttha Chinnarat, symbol of the province and one of the most distinguished Buddha images in the kingdom. Cast in the late Sukhothai period, about six centuries ago, the golden, flame-haloed image is extremely elegant and highly venerated.

✚ 8D ✉ 377km (234 miles) north of Bangkok

🍴 Excellent riverside restaurants 🚌 Buses from Bangkok 🚆 Phitsanulok Station ❓ Phitsanulok Boat Races, 16–17 Sep

ℹ 209/7–8 Thanon Borom Trailokanat ☎ 055 252 743

PHU HIN RONG KLA NATIONAL PARK

Between 1967 and 1982, Phu Hin Rong Kla was the headquarters of Thailand's communist insurgents, engaged in a protracted guerrilla war with Thai government forces based in and around Phitsanulok. A visit to the park makes a great day trip. The countryside en route is spectacular and visitors to the park can see the Red Flag Cliff, former Communist Party of Thailand headquarters, and other reminders of the struggle.

🕇 8D ✉ Park HQ 125km (78 miles) east of Phitsanulok ✋ Moderate 🍴 Vendors near the bungalows 🚌 Ordinary bus from Phitsanulok to Nakhon Thai, *songthaew* to park

SI SATCHANALAI

Si Satchanalai–Chaliang Historical Park is less visited than
Sukhothai but, arguably, more attractive. Dating from the 11th
century, the ruins are similar to those at Sukhothai, but less
restored and less immaculately kept, adding a mystique to the
atmosphere. If this early Thai kingdom fascinates you, be sure to
visit the former kilns at Sawankhalok, midway between Sukhothai
and Si Satchanalai. Further to the southwest the third ancient city
of the Sukhothai kingdom, Kamphaeng Phet, is undergoing major
restoration and is well worth a visit.

✚ 7C ✉ 70km (43 miles) north of Sukhothai ☎ 055 641 571 🍴 Restaurants
in nearby Sawankhalok 🚌 Regular air-conditioned buses from Sukhothai to
park entrance

SUKHOTHAI HISTORICAL PARK

See pages 52–53.

HOTELS

CHIANG MAI

Amari Rincome (BB)

Renowned for its reasonably priced lunch buffets and for promoting a wide range of international cuisines through regular food fairs. A good place for children.

✉ 1 Nimmanhaemin Road ☎ 053 221 123

Chiang Mai Plaza (BB)

Next to Chiang Mai's busy night bazaar area and close to the river. Live music in the coffee bar, often featuring popular musicians.

✉ 92 Thanon Si Donchai ☎ 053 270 036–50

Four Seasons Chiang Mai (BBB)

In the Mae Sa Valley surrounded by 8ha (20 acres) of landscaped gardens with lakes, rice fields and water buffaloes.

✉ Mae Rim–Samoeng Old Road, Chiang Mai ☎ 053 298 181; www.fourseasons.com/chiangmai

Lai Thai Guest House (B)

Good value, basic accommodation near the moat which surrounds Chiang Mai's old city. A perfect location if you happen to be in Chiang Mai during April's water-throwing festival.

✉ 111/4–5 Thanon Kotchasan ☎ 053 271 725

Montri (B)

This old Chiang Mai favourite has had a facelift and offers comfortable rooms at very reasonable rates.

✉ 2–6 Thanon Rachadamnoen (opposite the city's main gate, Pratu Tapei) ☎ 053 211 069; www.norththaihotel.com/montri.html

Rachamankha (BBB)

A Lanna-style hotel complex in a quiet corner of the old city, near its principal temple, Wat Phra Singh. Whitewashed walls, dark teak and low eaves give it a cool ambience in the summer heat.

✉ Thanon Rachamankha, Soi 9 ☎ 053 904 111; www.hotelrachamankha.com

Royal Princess (BB)

In the commercial heart of Chiang Mai. Popular with businesspeople, especially because of its Japanese and Chinese restaurants.

✉ 112 Thanon Chang Klan ☎ 053 281 033; www.royalprincess.com

Sheraton (BBB)

Chiang Mai's Sheraton (formerly the Westin Hotel) dominates the southern reaches of the city's Ping River, commanding sweeping views of the city and surrounding countryside.

✉ 318/1 Chiang Mai–Lamphun Road ☎ 053 275 300; www.sheratonhotels.com

Tamarind Village (BB)

A peaceful haven in the heart of the old city, with a secluded courtyard pool, terrace restaurant and a garden dominated by a beautiful old tamarind tree.

✉ 50/1 Thanon Rachadamnoen ☎ 053 418 900; www.tamarindvillage.com

CHIANG RAI

Dusit Island Resort (BB)

Large, luxurious hotel set on its own island in the middle of the Kok River. Plenty of local boat traffic makes for an interesting afternoon watching the passing parade.

✉ 1129 Thanon Kraisorasit ☎ 053 715 777

Golden Triangle Inn (B)

Attractive landscaped grounds include a Japanese-Thai garden. Room rates include an American breakfast. Also runs a helpful travel agency and car rental service.

✉ 590 Thanon Phahonyothin ☎ 053 716 996; www.chiangrai.dusit.com

Wangcome Hotel (BB)

In the heart of Chiang Rai. Comfortable rooms, coffee shop, disco and swimming pool.

✉ 869/90 Thanon Premawiphat ☎ 053 711 800; www.wangcome.com

GOLDEN TRIANGLE (SOP RUAK)
Anantara Golden Triangle (BBB)
Fabulous luxury resort using a mix of classic northern Thai forms and contemporary hotel design. Mountain biking, elephant rides, excursions and boat trips.

✉ 229 Moo 1 Golden Triangle, Sop Ruak ☎ 053 784 084; www.anantara.com

LAMPANG
Lampang Wiengthong Hotel (B)
A plush hotel in downtown Lampang, offering all the modern conveniences you would expect from a much more expensive place.

✉ 138/109 Thanon Phahonyothin ☎ 054 225 801; www.lampangweingthong.com

MAE HONG SON
Imperial Tara (BB)
A beautifully situated resort slightly to the south of the main town. Rooms are set amid tropical gardens and there is a good restaurant.

✉ 149 Moo 8, Tambon Pang Moo ☎ 053 611 272

NAN
Dheveraj Hotel (B)
Nan's largest and most modern hotel is popular with package tours, so can get quite noisy in high season. But it has all the usual tourist hotel comforts and the central courtyard is a pleasant place to relax on a warm evening.

✉ 466 Thanon Sumonthavaraj ☎ 054 710 078; www.dheverajhotel.com

Si Nuan Lodge (B)
Flowers from the owners' garden smother this pretty little brick-and-timber traditional Lanna-style property. Rooms are simply but charmingly furnished.

✉ 40 Thanon No Kharm, Tambol Nai Wiang ☎ 054 710 174 or 054 772 956

PHITSANULOK
Sappraiwan Grand Hotel and Resort (BB)
First-class resort with rooms ranging from singles to three-bedroom chalets. Set amid mountains on 120ha (296 acres) of landscaped grounds. Club house, fitness centre, paddle boats and more.

✉ 79 Moo 2, Tambon Kaengsopha, Amphur Wangthong ☎ 055 293 293; www.resort.co.th

Thani (BB)
Phitsanulok's newest hotel has a very high standard of comfort, with elegant rooms furnished in light woods and floral prints.

✉ 39 Thanon Sanambin ☎ 055 211 065–69; www.phitsanulokthani.com

SUKHOTHAI
Ananda Museum Gallery Hotel (BBB)
Sukhothai's newest and most luxuruous hotel is also a museum, displaying original, centuries-old pottery and fine reproductions, some of which decorate the rooms. The Celadon Garden restaurant guarantees fine dining in elegant surroundings.

✉ 10 Moo 4, Banlum, Sukhothai ☎ 055 622 428–31; www.ananda-hotel.com

Lotus Village (B)
A Frenchman and his Thai wife run this charming resort-style hotel-guesthouse, a short walk from central Sukhothai and its market. The breakfasts are truly Gallic, featuring very good coffee and delicious rolls.

✉ 170 Thanon Ratchathanee ☎ 055 621 484; www.lotus-village.com

RESTAURANTS

CHIANG MAI
Antique House (BB)
Superb northern Thai cooking near the Ping River, served amid antique Lanna furniture and handicrafts. Good central Thai food is also available. The restaurant has an early 20th–century feel.

✉ 71 Thanon Charoen Prathet ☎ 053 270 859 🕓 Lunch, dinner

La Casa (BB)

Chiang Mai's oldest Italian restaurant (founded 1988) is still probably the city's best, housed in a charming teak building on one of the main ring roads.

✉ 5 Irrigation Canal Road, Chiang Puak ☎ 053 215 802

Le Coq d'Or (BBB)

See page 58.

La Crystal (BBB)

Chiang Mai's newest French restaurant offers free transportation to guests from any hotel in the city and welcomes them with a complimentary cocktail. The elegant restaurant sits on the banks of the Ping River.

✉ 74/2 Thanon Paton, Amphoe Muang ☎ 053 872 890

The Gallery & Restaurant (BB)

You enter this romantic tree-shaded riverside restaurant through a courtyard gallery of exquisite antiques, which also leads into a café and cocktail bar, which is one of the city's best jazz haunts.

✉ 25–29 Thanon Charoenrat, Amphoe Muang ☎ 053 248 601

Old Chiang Mai Cultural Centre (BB)

Set in a series of old Lanna-style houses. Traditional northern-style *khantoke* dinners in peaceful surroundings, with classical dance and music.

✉ 185/3 Thanon Wualai ☎ 053 202 993–5 🕐 Dinner

Ratana's Kitchen (B)

You can choose from up to 300 dishes, Thai and Western, at this café-style little restaurant on Chiang Mai's main thoroughfare, Thanon Tapei. A few rustic tables outside allow for fine-weather dining.

✉ 320–322 Thanon Tapei ☎ 053 874 173 🕐 Breakfast, lunch, dinner

Riverside (BB)

See page 59.

CHIANG RAI
Cham Cha (B)
Conveniently located next to Chiang Rai's tourist office, this simple Thai restaurant serves excellent Lanna-style dishes, but select a table upstairs to avoid the crowds.

✉ Thanon Singhaklai ☎ 053 744 191

Hawnariga (B)
This thatch-roofed, open-sided restaurant takes its name from the nearby *Hawnariga* (clock tower), a local landmark. Orchids hang from the eaves and a small stream runs through the dining area, where very tasty Thai food is served by a friendly staff.

✉ 402/1–2 Thanon Banpapragarn ☎ 053 711 062

DOI MAE SALONG
Mae Salong Villa (BB)
Yunnanese Chinese dishes in the best restaurant in town. Spectacular views across the valley. Warm up with a fruit liqueur.

✉ 5 Mu 1, Santikhiri ☎ 053 765 115 🕐 Lunch, dinner

GOLDEN TRIANGLE (SOP RUAK)
Border View (BB)
See page 58.

KAMPHAENG PHET
Ruan Phae Rim Ping (BB)
Beautiful garden restaurant beside the Ping River. Good central Thai cuisine including kai phat pet mamuang (fried chicken with cashew nuts).

✉ Soi 1 Thanon Thesa 2 ☎ 055 712 767 🕐 Lunch, dinner

LAMPANG
Riverside Bar and Restaurant (BB)
Excellent Thai food on the banks of the Yom River. Live Thai folk music most nights.

✉ 328 Thanon Tipchang ☎ 054 221 861 🕐 Lunch, dinner

MAE HONG SON
Bai Fern (BB)
Mostly Thai food with some simple Western dishes. One of the best places in town.

✉ Thanon Khunlum Praphat ☎ 053 611 374 🕐 Lunch, dinner

Golden Teak Restaurant (BB)
Part of the Imperial Tara complex. Good Western food.

✉ 149 Moo 8, Tambon Pang Moo ☎ 053 684 444 🕐 Breakfast, lunch, dinner

MAE SAI
Rabieng Kaew (BB)
Pleasant garden restaurant serving good central and northern Thai food and regional dishes such as Korean barbecued beef.

✉ 356/2 Moo 1 Thanon Paholyothin ☎ 053 731 172–3 🕐 Breakfast, lunch, dinner

NAN
Da Dario (BB)
Extensive range of well-prepared, authentic Italian dishes. Friendly staff and atmosphere.

✉ 37/4 Thanon Rajamnuay, Ban Prakerd ☎ 054 750 258 🕐 Lunch, dinner

Siam Pochana (B)
An old wooden building housing the most reliable restaurant in Nan. Menu is all Thai and Chinese. Try the jok rice porridge for breakfast.

✉ Thanon Sumon Dheveraj ☎ No telephone 🕐 Breakfast, lunch, dinner

PHITSANULOK
Rim Nan (BB)
A floating restaurant moored by the west bank of the Nan River. Pleasant ambience and cool breezes in the hot season. The house special is neua yang (barbecued beef) 'Genghis Khan'.

✉ 63/2 Thanon Wang Chan ☎ 055 251 446 🕐 Lunch, dinner

SUKHOTHAI
Dream Café and Antique House (BB)
Decorated with 19th- and early 20th-century Thai antiques, this place has character. Thai, Chinese and Western dishes are served here, plus many herbal liqueurs.

✉ 86/1 Thanon Singhawat ☎ 055 612 081 🕓 Lunch, dinner

SHOPPING

BOOKS AND CDS
DK Book House
Cultural books on Thailand, Burma and Laos.

✉ 7/1 Thanon Kotchasan, Chiang Mai ☎ 053 206 995

Lost Bookshop
Second-hand novels, biographies and art books.

✉ 34/3 Thanon Ratchamankha, Chiang Mai

Suriwong Book Centre
Stationery, guidebooks and books on Southeast Asia.

✉ 54/1–5 Thanon Sri Donchai, Chiang Mai ☎ 053 281 052

GEMS AND JEWELLERY
Jolie Femme
A large showroom plus a silk factory where you can watch the complete process of silk manufacture under one roof.

✉ 8/3 Chiang Mai–San Kamphaeng Road, Chiang Mai ☎ 053 247 222

Nova Collection
A gallery and school with courses in jewellery production.

✉ 201 Thanon Tapae, Chiang Mai ☎ 053 273 058

Royal Orchid Collection
Real orchids, roses and other flowers are set in gold and silver plate by the craftsmen and women of this unique local enterprise.

✉ 2nd floor, 94–120 Thanon Charoen Muang, Chiang Mai ☎ 053 245 598

Sherry Silverware
Fine silver from Chiang Mai workshops, at very reasonable prices.
✉ 59/2 Thanon Loi Kroh, Chiang Mai ☎ 053 273 529

Shiraz Co Ltd
Reputable dealer, selling all types of gems and jewellery. Buy from stock or order to suit.
✉ 170 Thanon Tapae, Chiang Mai ☎ 053 252 382

ENTERTAINMENT

BARS AND NIGHTCLUBS

Bubbles Disco
An evergreen on the Chiang Mai night scene, popular with Thais and foreigners.
✉ Pornping Tower Hotel, 46–8 Thanon Charoen Prathet, Chiang Mai
☎ 053 270 099 ⊙ Daily 9pm–2am

Riverside
A large riverside bar and restaurant with two live bands nightly.
✉ 9/11 Thanon Charoen Rat, Chiang Mai ☎ 053 243 239 ⊙ Daily 10am–1.30am

SPORT

Chiang Mai Sky Adventure
Offers microlight flights giving splendid views of the historic city of Chiang Mai. Trips last either 15 or 30 minutes and you are welcome to bring your camera along.
✉ 143 Moo 6, Chiang Doi, Amphur Doi Saket, Chiang Mai ☎ 053 868 460

Gymkhana Club
The second oldest sports club in Southeast Asia houses squash and tennis courts, as well as a beautiful nine-hole golf course.
✉ Chiang Mai–Lamphun Road, Chiang Mai ☎ 053 241 035

Lanna Sports Club
A 27-hole golf course with tennis and badminton courts, horse-back riding and an excellent fitness centre, including a swimming pool.
✉ KM1 Thanon Chotana, Chiang Mai ☎ 053 221 911 🕐 Tee off 6

The Peak
Situated next door to Chiang Mai's famous Night Bazaar, The Peak offers visitors the chance to test their mountaineering skills on a challenging man-made cliff.
✉ Night Market, Thanon Chang Klan, Chiang Mai ☎ 053 820 776–8
🕐 Daily 2–11

Thai Adventure Rafting
Two-day rafting adventures on the Pai River. The trips pass throug scenic wilderness taking in waterfalls, gorges and the thrill of the rapids.
✉ 73/7 Charoen Prathet (near the Diamond Riverside Hotel), Chiang Mai
☎ 053 277 178

Velocity Cycle Hire and Tours
Chiang Mai's quiet roads leading off into the hills are perfect for avid cyclists. Bikes can be rented from this shop.
✉ 177 Thanon Changpuek, Sripoom, Chiang Mai ☎ 053 410 665

Isaan

Thailand's least-developed area, the great northeastern region comprising the Khorat Plateau and Mekong Valley, is worth visiting for its many attractions and the locals' engaging disposition. The people are Thai nationals whose mother tongue is Lao. They have a distinctive musical tradition and a spicy cuisine, loved by Thais. The Khorat Plateau is an immense, semi-arid tableland punctuated by the cities of Nakhon Ratchasima (also known as Khorat), Khon Kaen, Ubon Ratchathani and Udon Thani. The 'Khmer Culture Trail' – a jewel-like string of Khmer temples dating from the Angkor period – leads east from Nakhon Ratchasima to a point near Ubon Ratchathani.

The Mekong Valley is a lush region of green rice paddies, fishing villages and riverside market towns. Almost the entire west bank of the great river is driveable, and the influences of Vietnam, Cambodia and Laos are palpable in riverine settlements. Since 1994 the river has been bridged at Nong Khai by the Mittraphap or 'Friendship' Bridge, the main gateway to the nearby Lao capital of Vientiane.

BAN CHIANG

The small upper Isaan village of Ban Chiang is the site of one of the oldest known cultures in Southeast Asia. As early as 2000BC people living in the vicinity were firing elegantly patterned clay pots. Now a UNESCO World Heritage Site, the village is

worth visiting to see the excavations, **Ban Chiang Museum** and examples of the early bronze objects produced by Ban Chiang culture. Although not necessarily related to the original potters, the present inhabitants of the village have taken up the trade with enthusiasm and produce attractive and inexpensive imitations.

10D ✉ 50km (31 miles) east of Udon Thani 🚌 *Songthaew* from Udon Thani

Ban Chiang Museum

🕐 Daily 9–4 💵 Inexpensive

CHONABOT

The small town of Chonabot is renowned for its weaving, particularly its *mat-mii* tie-dyed cotton and silk. A stroll almost anywhere in the village will lead past wooden houses raised on stilts, with local womenfolk weaving in the shade underneath. The best place to gain an overall impression of this upper Isaan art form is at the local handicraft centre on Thanon Pho Sii Sa-aat in the northern part of town. Here, in addition to silk and cotton cloth, ceramics and other assorted local handicrafts are for sale.

10E ✉ 50km (31 miles) southwest of Khon Kaen 🕐 Centre: daily 9–6 🚌 *Songthaew* from Khon Kaen ❓ Silk Fair, Khon Kaen, last week Nov–first week Dec

CHONG MEK AND THE EMERALD TRIANGLE

The southeastern part of Isaan, around and beyond the Sirindhon Reservoir, is being quietly promoted by the Tourism Authority of Thailand as the 'Emerald Triangle', an Isaan equivalent to the 'Golden Triangle' of the north. Here, where the borders of Laos, Cambodia and Thailand meet, is some lovely unspoiled countryside including Kaeng Tana National Park. In August 2000 a new bridge across the Mekong River at Pakse was completed and the road via Chong Mek became the gateway to southern Laos.

➕ 12F ✉ 75km (45 miles) east of Ubon Ratchathani 🍴 Food stalls at border post 🚌 Bus from Ubon to Phibun Mangsahan, *songthaew* from Phibun

KHAO PHRA VIHARN

This massive, magnificent, 800-year-old Khmer temple, seated on a high escarpment of the Dongrek Mountains, lies across the frontier within Cambodian territory (where it is known as Preah Vihear) but is only accessible from Thailand. Visitors can cross into Cambodia without a visa by paying the B100 entry charge, leaving their passport and proceeding across the frontier on foot. It is a steep climb but worth it. The view across the Cambodian plain, about 200m (218 yds) below, is breathtaking.

➕ 11F ✉ 106km (66 miles) south of Si Sa Ket 🕐 Daily 6–6 🍴 Food stalls before Thai border point 🚌 *Songthaew* from Si Sa Ket ✋ Moderate

KHONG CHIAM

This small settlement at the confluence of the Mun and Mekong rivers provides a quiet base for visitors wishing to explore the Emerald Triangle. Located on a picturesque peninsula between the two rivers, it is a good place for boating or fishing on the Mekong. Comfortable hotel and bungalow accommodation is available. About 20km (12 miles) north is the overhanging cliff of Pha Taem, featuring prehistoric paintings of people, fish, elephants and turtles estimated to be at least three millennia old. Views from the top of the cliff across the Mekong to Laos are spectacular.

➕ 12E ✉ 74km (46 miles) east of Ubon Ratchathani 🍴 Floating restaurants on the Mun River 🚌 Ordinary buses from Ubon Ratchathani

NAKHON RATCHASIMA

The second largest city in Thailand, although much smaller than Bangkok, is the gateway to the northeast. Featuring good restaurants and accommodation, it is an ideal base for exploring Phimai. Mahawirawong National Museum has a good collection of early Khmer carvings and sculpture. In the middle of town stands a shrine to Thao Suranari (also known as Khunying Mo), a local heroine who helped defeat a Lao invasion of Nakhon Ratchasima in the early 19th century.

➕ 9F ✉ 250km (155 miles) northeast of Bangkok 🍴 Good Chinese restaurants 🚌 Buses from Bangkok 🚆 Nakhon Ratchasima ✈ Nakhon Ratchasima ❓ End of Mar–early Apr

NONG KHAI

This pleasant riverside town is the jumping-off point for visits to nearby Laos, especially the Lao capital, Vientiane. Such visits had to be made by ferry until 1994, when the Mittraphap or 'Friendship' Bridge opened. Nong Khai is a quiet town with some attractive Sino-French architecture along Thanon Meechai. In the hot season (March to May), watch out for Phra That Klang Nam,

'the Holy Reliquary in the Midst of the River' – the remains of a Buddhist temple that slipped into the Mekong in 1850 and are visible only when the river runs at its lowest.

✚ 10C ✉ 620km (384 miles) northeast of Bangkok 🍴 Banya Pochana (BB) 🚌 Regular air-conditioned buses from Bangkok 🚉 Nong Khai

PRASAT PHANOM RUNG

See pages 48–49.

PRASAT HIN PHIMAI

This remarkable Khmer temple was constructed in the late 10th to early 11th centuries as part of a network of Khmer religious structures connected with Angkor. Built of white and pink sandstone, the complex has been restored and, along with Phanom Rung, is one of the two finest Khmer temples outside Cambodia. The new Phimai National Museum, nearby, is highly recommended. There is also a vast banyan tree – looking more like a small forest than a single tree – where visitors can have their fortune told.

✚ 10F ✉ 58km (36 miles) northeast of Nakhon Ratchasima 🕓 Historical Park daily 7.30–6 ✋ Inexpensive 🚌 1305 from Nakhon Ratchasima ❓ Phimai Long-Boat Races and Festival

SURIN

For most of the year this quiet provincial capital lies off the beaten track. However, a carnival atmosphere pervades in November during the Surin Elephant Round-up, which is so popular that visitors must book in advance. Most of the local people, known as Suay, speak a variant of Khmer (as well as Thai) and are known for their skill with elephants.

✚ 10F ✉ 452km (280 miles) northeast of Bangkok
🍴 Wang Petch (BB) 🚌 Buses from Bangkok
🚆 Surin Station

UBON RATCHATHANI

Although one of Thailand's larger cities, Ubon Ratchathani is a long way from Bangkok and consequently rather off the tourist map. This is a pity, as it's an attractive, friendly, laid-back place that deserves more visitors. It is also a convenient base for exploring the Emerald Triangle, the Mekong River at Khong Jiam and Khao Phra Viharn.

Tucked away in the southeastern corner of lower Isaan, Ubon has long been defined as 'the end of the line' from Bangkok. This is changing, however, after the reopening of the ancient Khmer temple of Khao Phra Viharn just across the Cambodian border, and the completion of a new bridge across the Mekong at Pakse, in nearby Laos. Far from being the end of the line, Ubon is set to become the gateway to southern Laos and central Vietnam. The city was home to an important US airbase during the Vietnam War but today is a quieter place, holding an annual candle festival in July and boasting a fine museum.

➕ 12F ✉ 630km (391 miles) northeast of Bangkok 🍴 Good Chinese and Vietnamese restaurants 🚌 Regular air-conditioned buses from Bangkok 🚆 Warin Chamrap Station ✈ Ubon Ratchathani Airport

HOTELS

BURIRAM (PHANOM RUNG)
Grand Hotel (B)
It hardly lives up to its name, but Buriram's Grand Hotel is
nevertheless among the best in town and offers a reasonable
standard of comfort. Rooms have TV, a fridge and fans or
air-conditioning.
✉ Corner of Thanon Nivas and Thanon Plat Muang ☎ 044 611 179

KHON KAEN
Sofitel Raja Orchid (BBB)
The northeast's most luxurious hotel with restaurants serving Thai,
Italian and Vietnamese food. Large underground entertainment
complex and disco.
✉ 9/9 Thanon Prachasamran ☎ 043 322 155; www.sofitelkhonkaen.com

LOEI
Thai Udom (B)
Adequate facilities in a typical up-country Thai hotel. Probably
better than anywhere else in Loei, and a good base to explore
nearby Phu Kradung National Park.
✉ Thanon Charoenrat ☎ 042 811 763

MUKDAHAN
Mukdahan Grand (B)
The best accommodation in Mukdahan. Offers tours to the Lao
city of Savannakhet.
✉ 78 Thanon Songnang Sathit ☎ 042 612 020

NAKHON RATCHASIMA (KHORAT)
Royal Princess Khorat (BB)
Decorated in northeastern Thai style, this first-class hotel has a
large pool, business centre and the famed Empress Chinese
restaurant.
✉ 1137 Thanon Suranari ☎ 044 256 629–35; www.dusit.com

Sima Thani (BB)
The top hotel in town is some distance from the main action.
All rooms have satellite television, and are clean and spacious.
✉ Thanon Mittraphap ☎ 044 213 100; www.simathani.com

NONG KHAI
Mekong Royal Nong Khai (BB)
Near the Friendship Bridge, which spans the Mekong between
Thailand and Laos, this luxury hotel has the best accommodation
in town. Pool and coffee shop.
✉ 222 Thanon Had Jommani ☎ 042 420 024

SURIN
Thong Tarin (B)
Surin's best hotel with economic room rates that include a buffet
breakfast. Large massage parlour.
✉ 60 Thanon Sirirat ☎ 044 514 281–8

UBON RATCHATHANI
Regent Palace (B)
Large, comfortable, provincial hotel with cocktail lounge, coffee
shop, in-room satellite television and snooker hall.
✉ 265–271 Thanon Chayangkun ☎ 045 262 920–4

UDON THANI
Charoen (B)
Large hotel, with a budget old wing and a more expensive new
wing. Great facilities including disco, cocktail lounge and pool.
✉ 549 Thanon Phosri ☎ 042 248 155; www.udonthani.com/charoen

Gecko Villa (BBB)
Owned by local villagers, this peaceful villa, surrounded by rice
fields, is perfect for travellers seeking to experience Thailand away
from the tourist trail. Activites such as Thai cooking courses,
fishing and helping to harvest rice with the locals can be arranged.
✉ 20km (12 miles) southeast of Udon Thani ☎ 019 180 500;
www.geckovilla.com

RESTAURANTS

CHIANG KHAN
Mekong Riverside (B)
A beautiful setting with views over the river to Laos. A good place for a cool drink at sunset.
✉ Soi 10 Thanon Chai Khong ☎ No telephone 🕐 Lunch, dinner

KHON KAEN
Khrua Weh (BB)
Genuine Vietnamese food plus excellent Thai and Isaan dishes served in an attractive old teak house. Try the spicy chicken and mint salad.
✉ 1/1 Thanon Klang Meuang ☎ No telephone 🕐 Lunch, dinner

Parrot Restaurant (B)
Offers an extensive menu including pizza, hamburgers and a good selection of Thai dishes. Good service.
✉ Thanon Sri Chan ☎ 043 244 692 🕐 Breakfast, lunch, dinner

LOEI
Sawita Bakery (B)
A coffee shop that also serves good central Thai food and Western fast food like burgers and spaghetti. A good range of cakes.
✉ 139 Thanon Charoenrat ☎ No telephone 🕐 Breakfast, lunch, dinner

MUKDAHAN
Riverside (BB)
Situated on the Mekong, this shady terrace offers mainly Thai and Chinese dishes. Perfect in the late afternoon with a cold beer.
✉ Thanon Samran Chai Khong ☎ 042 612 846 🕐 Breakfast, lunch, dinner

NAKHON PHANOM
Golden Giant Catfish (B)
Riverside restaurant specializing in the giant Mekong catfish, which can weigh up to 200kg (440lb).
✉ Thanon Sunthon Vichit ☎ 042 511 218 🕐 Breakfast, lunch, dinner

NAKHON RATCHASIMA
Bankaew (BB)
Luxurious establishment specializing in seafood.
✉ 105/17–19 Thanon Jomsurangyat ☎ 044 246 512 ◷ Breakfast, lunch, dinner

VFW Café (B)
Founded by ex-US servicemen who stayed on after the Vietnam War. Serves steaks, sausages and pizzas.
✉ 167–8 Thanon Phoklang ☎ 044 253 432 ◷ Breakfast, lunch, dinner

NONG KHAI
Banya Pochana (BB)
Serves Thai, Chinese and Lao food and specializes in fish dishes. Beautiful views across the Mekong to the Mittraphap Bridge and Laos.
✉ 295 Thanon Rim Khong ☎ No telephone ◷ Lunch, dinner

PHANOM RUNG
Phanom Rung Historical Park (B)
The only place to eat at Phanom Rung. A series of stalls and small restaurants offering Isaan food like papaya salad, grilled chicken, curries and sticky rice.
✉ Phanom Rung Hill ☎ No telephone ◷ Breakfast, lunch

PHIMAI
Baitoey (B)
Good Thai and Western fare in a pleasant rustic setting. Menu includes vegetarian dishes, ice cream and various sticky rice and coconut sweets.
✉ Thanon Jomsudah Sadet ☎ No telephone ◷ Breakfast, lunch, dinner

SURIN
Wang Petch (BB)
Wide range of Thai, Chinese and Western dishes. Surin's most trendy restaurant, geared to businesspeople. Live music nightly.
✉ 104 Thanon Jitbumrung ☎ 044 511 274 ◷ Breakfast, lunch, dinner

THAT PHANOM
Somkhane (B)
Near the triumphal arch in the central area, this small restaurant offers great Thai and Chinese fish dishes.

✉ Thanon Kuson Ratchadamnoen 🕐 Breakfast, lunch, dinner

UBON RATCHATHANI
Chiokee (B)
The place to visit for a good breakfast, be it Western-style or Thai-style. A special is congee (jok), a thick porridge served with an egg and minced pork.

✉ Thanon Kheuan Thani 🕐 Breakfast, lunch

Indochine (BB)
See page 58.

Sincere Restaurant (BB)
Tastefully decorated establishment serving fine French and Thai food. Owner and chef Khun Panee ran a French restaurant in Pattaya before retiring to Ubon.

✉ 126/1 Thanon Sappasit ☎ 045 245 061 🕐 Lunch, dinner; closed Sun

UDON THANI
Ban Isaan (B)
Serves all the northeast's best-known dishes. First-rate spicy minced chicken and mint leaves (laap kai) and green papaya salad (som tam).

✉ 177–179 Thanon Adunyadet ☎ No telephone 🕐 Lunch, dinner

Rung Thong (B)
One of the oldest restaurants in Isaan, known for its excellent curries. Also serves central and northeastern dishes.

✉ Thanon Prajak Silpakorn, west of the Clock Tower ☎ No telephone
🕐 Lunch, dinner

Steve's Bar (BB)

Local ex-pats, including some Vietnam War and CIA veterans, frequent this centrally located, friendly bar. The kitchen serves a mixture of Thai dishes and simple Western fare.

✉ Thanon Prajaksilapakon ☎ 042 244 523

Udom Rot (B)

Overlooks the ferry crossing point to Laos. Dishes include Vietnamese-style spring rolls, Isaan minced meats (laap) and very good freshwater fish dishes.

✉ 193 Thanon Rim Khong ☎ No telephone ◷ Breakfast, lunch, dinner

SHOPPING

MARKETS, ANTIQUES AND HANDICRAFTS

Suun Silapahattakam Pheun Baan

This handicraft centre in Chonabot sells the locally produced *matmii* silk, justly famous throughout Thailand and beyond.

✉ Thanon Pho Sii Sa-aat, Chonabot, Khon Kaen

Village Weaver Handicrafts

A fabric centre specializing in beautifully woven items, including ready-to-wear clothing. Also excellent hand-dyed cotton.

✉ 786/1 Thanon Prajak, Nong Khai

SHOPPING CENTRES

Big C

Big C shopping complexes can be found in many of the larger central and northeast towns. This one has a good supermarket and plenty of small eating places, including the usual American fast-food outlets.

✉ Thanon Mittaphap, Nakhon Ratchasima

Index

Acknowledgements

The Automobile Association would like to thank the following photographers, companies and picture libraries for their assistance in the preparation of this book.

Abbreviations for the picture credits are as follows – (t) top; (b) bottom; (c) centre; (l) left; (r) right; (AA) AA World Travel Library.

6/7 Grand Palace, AA/D Henley; **8/9** Monk, AA/J Holmes; **10/11** Tourists on beach, AA/D Henley; **10c** Buddha head, AA/D Henley; **10bl** Buddha statue, AA/D Henley; **10br** Buddhist monks, AA/J Holmes; **11c** Lotus flower, AA/J Holmes; **11b** Fishing boat, AA/D Henley; **12** Market, AA/J Holmes; **12/3** Food stall, AA/J Holmes; **13** Fish, AA/D Henley; **14tl** Rambutans, AA/J Holmes; **14b** Crab, AA/J Holmes; **14/5t** Aubergines, AA/D Henley; **14/5b** Chillies, AA/J Holmes; **15** Squid stall, AA/J Holmes; **16** Grand Palace, AA/D Henley; **16/7t** Phang-Nga Bay, AA/D Henley; **17l** Buddha, AA/J Holmes; **17r** Thai dish; AA/D Henley; **18** Classical dancer, AA/J Holmes; **18/9** Khao Phra Viharn, AA/J Holmes; **19** Rice for sale, AA/J Holmes; **20/1** Traffic, AA/D Henley; **24/5** Festival, AA/J Holmes; **26/7** Airport, AA/D Henley; **27** Train, AA/J Holmes; **28** Ferry, AA/J Holmes; **30** Telephone AA/J Holmes; **32** Policeman, AA/D Henley; **34/5** Sukhothai Historical Park, AA/J Holmes; **36/7t** Chatuchak Weekend Market AA/D Henley; **36/7b** Chatuchuk Weekend Market, AA/D Henley; **37** Chatuchuk Weekend Market, AA/D Henley; **38/9** Doi Inthanon, AA/D Henley; **39** (inset) Doi Inthanon, AA/D Henley; **40** Grand Palace, AA/D Henley; **40/1t** Grand Palace, AA/D Henley; **40/1b** Grand Palace, AA/D Henley; **42** Khao Sok National Park, AA/D Henley; **42/3** Khao Sok National Park, AA/D Henley; **44** Mekong River, AA/J Holmes; **44/5** Mekong River, AA/D Henley; **46/7** Muslim fishing village on Panyi Island, AA/D Henley; **47** Phang-nga Bay, AA/R Strange; **48/9** Prasat Phanom Rung, AA/B Davies; **49** Prasat Phanom Rung, AA/R Strange; **50/1t** Similan Islands, AA/D Henley; **50/1b** Similan Islands, AA/D Henley; **52** Sukhothai Historical Park, AA/J Holmes; **52/3** Sukhothai Historical Park, AA/J Holmes; **53** Sukhothai Historical Park; AA/J Holmes; **54/5** Wat Phra That Lampang Luang, AA/D Henley; **56/7** Erawan National Park, AA/ D Henley; **58/9** Restaurant, AA/J Holmes; **60/1** Market, AA/J Holmes; **62/3** Elephant conservation centre, AA/D Henley; **64** Diving boat, AA/D Henley; **64/5** Rock climbing, AA/D Henley; **66/7** View from Doi Suthep, AA/J Holmes; **69** Night Bazaar, AA/D Henley; **70/1** Queen Saovabha Memorial Institute (Snake farm), AA/J Holmes; **73** Ko Phangan, AA/D Henley; **74/5** Thai dishes, AA/D Henley; **76** Wat Arun, AA/R Strange; **76/7** Wat Arun, AA/ R Strange; **78/9** Doi Inthanon National Park, AA/D Henley; **80/1** National museum in Phetchaburi, AA/J Holmes; **82/3** Elephant rides, AA/D Henley; **85** Floating market at Damnoen Saduak, AA/R Strange; **86/7** Chinatown, AA/J Holmes; **87** Long boat on canal in Bangkok, AA/J Holmes; **88/9** Bang Khu Wiang Floating Market, AA/R Strange; **90** Wat Mangkon Kamalawat, AA/ J Holmes; **90/1** Chinatown, AA/J Holmes; **92** Khao San Road, AA/J Holmes; **92/3** National Museum, AA/J Holmes; **93** Jim Thompson's House, AA/D Henley; **94** Oriental Hotel, AA/J Holmes; **95** Ayutthaya, AA/R Strange; **96/7** Ayutthaya, AA/D Henley; **97** Ayutthaya, AA/D Henley; **98t** Chanthaburi, AA/D Henley; **98b** Damnoen Saduak Floating Market, AA/D Henley; **99** Ko Chang, AA/D Henley; **100** Erawan National Park, AA/D Henley; **100/1** Kamphaeng Phet Historical Park, AA/D Henley; **101** JEATH War Museum, AA/D Henley; **102/3** River Kwai, AA/D Henley; **104t** Ko Chang, AA/D Henley; **104b** Shrine on Ko Samet, AA/D Henley; **105** Phra Pathom Chedi, AA/D Henley; **106/7** Lopburi, AA/D Henley; **108** Karen people, AA/D Henley; **123** Krabi, AA/D Henley; **124/5** Phuket, AA/D Henley; **126** Patong Beach in Phuket, AA/D Henley; **126/7** Fishing boats, AA/J Holmes; **129** Phra Ratchaniwet Marukhathaiyawan Palace, AA/J Holmes; **130** Ko Samui, AA/D Henley; **131** Craftsman in Ko Samui, AA/J Holmes; **132** Monks hut in Krabi, AA/D Henley; **133** Hat Tham Phra Nang, AA/D Henley; **134/5** Monk, AA/D Henley; **136t** Pattani, AA/D Henley; **136b** Lantern in Chinese temple in Pattani, AA/D Henley; **137** Prachuap Khiri Khan, AA/R Strange; **138** Songkhla, AA/D Henley; **147** Chiang Saen, AA/J Holmes; **148** Chiang Mai, AA/D Henley; **149** Baw Sang Umbrella Village, AA/J Holmes; **150/1** Wat Phrathat Doi Suthep, AA/D Henley; **151** Lampang, AA/D Henley; **152** Lamphun, AA/D Henley; **153** Night Bazaar, AA/D Henley; **154** Chiang Rai, AA/D Henley; **155** Chiang Rai, AA/D Henley; **156** Chiang Saen museum, AA/J Holmes; **156/7** Mae Hong Son, AA/D Henley; **158** Mae Sai, AA/R Strange; **158/9** Wat Phumin in Nan, AA/D Henley; **160** Phitsanulok, AA/R Strange; **160/1** Phu Hin Rong Kla National Park, AA/R Strange; **162** Si Satchanalai, AA/D Henley; **173** Relief at Wat in Ubon Ratchathani, AA/D Henley; **174** Relief in Ban Chiang, AA/J Holmes; **174/5** Ban Chiang, AA/J Holmes; **176** Monk at Khao Phra Viharn, AA/J Holmes; **177** Khao Phra Viharn, AA/J Holmes; **178** Shrine of Thao Suranari in Nakhon Ratchasima, AA/J Holmes; **178/9** Nong Khai, AA/J Holmes; **180** Surin, AA/J Holmes; **180/1** Surin, AA/J Holmes; **181** School children in Ubon Ratchathani, AA/J Holmes.

Questionnaire

Dear Traveler

Your comments, opinions and recommendations are very important to us. So please help us to improve our travel guides by taking a few minutes to complete this simple questionnaire.

Send to: Essential Guides,
MailStop 64, 1000 AAA Drive, Heathrow, FL 32746–5063

Your recommendations...

We always encourage readers' recommendations for restaurants, nightlife or shopping – if your recommendation is added to the next edition of the guide, we will send you a FREE AAA Essential Guide of your choice. Please state below the establishment name, location and your reasons for recommending it.

_____

_____

_____

_____

_____

Please send me AAA Essential _____

About this guide...

Which title did you buy?

_____ **AAA Essential**

Where did you buy it? _____

When? m m / y y

Why did you choose a AAA Essential Guide? _____

_____

_____

_____

Did this guide meet with your expectations?

Exceeded ☐   Met all ☐   Met most ☐   Fell below ☐

Please give your reasons _____

_____

_____

_____

continued on next page...

Were there any aspects of this guide that you particularly liked? _____

_____

_____

_____

_____

Is there anything we could have done better? _____

_____

_____

_____

_____

_____

About you...

Name (Mr/Mrs/Ms) _____

Address _____

_____

_____ Zip _____

Daytime tel nos. _____

Which age group are you in?

Under 25 ☐ 25–34 ☐ 35–44 ☐ 45–54 ☐ 55–64 ☐ 65+ ☐

How many trips do you make a year?

Less than one ☐ One ☐ Two ☐ Three or more ☐

Are you a AAA member? Yes ☐ No ☐

Name of AAA club _____

About your trip

When did you book? m m / y y   When did you travel? m m / y y

How long did you stay? _____

Was it for business or leisure? _____

Did you buy any other travel guides for your trip? Yes ☐ No ☐

If yes, which ones? _____

Thank you for taking the time to complete this questionnaire.